SpringerBriefs in Law

More information about this series at http://www.springer.com/series/10164

Elena D'Agostino

Contracts of Adhesion Between Law and Economics

Rethinking the Unconscionability Doctrine

Springer

Elena D'Agostino
Department of Economics, Business,
Environmental and Quantitative Methods
University of Messina
Messina
Italy

ISSN 2192-855X ISSN 2192-8568 (electronic)
ISBN 978-3-319-13113-9 ISBN 978-3-319-13114-6 (eBook)
DOI 10.1007/978-3-319-13114-6

Library of Congress Control Number: 2014954618

Springer Cham Heidelberg New York Dordrecht London

Printed on acid-free paper

Springer is part of Springer Science+Business Media (www.springer.com)

Contents

Chapter 1
The Unconscionability Doctrine in a Law and Economics Perspective

1.1 What Is a Contract of Adhesion?

A contract is a legally binding agreement between two or more parties enforced by law in light of a mutual consensus that parties show by signing. Then, in a traditional (according to Korobkin (2003), "Platonic") view, a contract is defined as "a meeting of minds"[1] in order to emphasize parties' common understanding of its content in the course of its formation. This condition, well known among lawyers as "awareness," is a necessary requirement[2] to the correct formation of any bilateral agreement including contracts.[3] In this sense, any contract is also the final result of a bargaining process in which parties should not fight each other, but rather have to coordinate their opposite interests in order to reach an agreement.[4] To do so, parties are expected to communicate in order to discuss what clauses to include.

In the hypothetical Coasian world, transactions are costless and allow people to reach an efficient solution. By contrast, in the real world, transactions are expensive,

---

[1] This expression was used in Baltimore and Ohio R. Co. v. United States (1923) where the US Supreme Court stated that a contract is "an agreement … founded upon a meeting of minds, which, although not embodied in an express contract, is inferred, as a fact, from conduct of the parties showing, in the light of the surrounding circumstances, their tacit understanding."

[2] Even though rules may change from country to country, other requirements for a contract to be enforceable are usually: (1) competent parties: it excludes enforceability whenever one party is drugged, mentally impaired or minor; (2) consideration: if a party gives something, the others must give something else back; (3) legal purpose: a contract which requires one party to violate the law is not valid; (4) legal form: some contracts must have a specific form or be drawn in a certain way, according with law requirements.

[3] According to the traditional doctrine, there is no meeting of minds if: (1) one side is joking; (2) there is a misunderstanding about some essential element; (3) both sides have made a material mistake about some clauses.

[4] On the concept of bargaining as coordination, See Schelling (1960).

E. D'Agostino, *Contracts of Adhesion Between Law and Economics*,
SpringerBriefs in Law, DOI 10.1007/978-3-319-13114-6_1

especially in a globalized mass production economy with a large number of individual consumers, where parties might not be physically present and communication turns out impossible or, at least, highly expensive. The main example in this sense is given by Internet transactions, even though transactions between distant parties have characterized trading also in the past (see Slawson 1971). For that reason, consumers are usually asked to put signatures on preprinted contracts, usually referred to as "contracts of adhesion."

Using such expressions lawyers refer to those contracts (1) presented by sellers to consumers in a take-it-or-leave-it form and (2) containing standard clauses. The first feature emphasizes the unequal bargaining power between parties where the drafter is usually involved in many transactions of the same type with several different consumers; while the consumer is usually involved in an occasional transaction. About the second feature, since consumers do not take any role in the negotiation process, it turns out that each seller proposes the same contract with the same clauses to each customer, so that contracts are usually standard.

Examples of contracts of adhesion are very common nowadays in transactions such as contracts of transportation, bank contracts, credit card issuing or account opening, insurance policies and so on.

Coase (1960) might comment that contracts of adhesion reduce high transaction costs existing in several markets, like those cited above, simply to the cost of writing the contract (endured by the drafter party) and to the cost of reading the contract (endured by the nondrafter party). In this sense, a contract of adhesion is not necessarily a bad contract except for the risk that the drafter can exploit his higher power by including some clauses turning out favorable to himself only and unfavorable to consumers. In order to take consumers' attention away from those clauses whose content might negatively influence their purchasing decisions, they are usually "hidden" in fine print or positioned at the bottom of the contract or even in some annexes, and are written in an obscure language, difficult for ordinary consumers to understand, and usually called pejoratively "boilerplate."

Following the Ben-Shahar's (2005) definition, "boilerplate (…) are the building blocks of standard form, nonnegotiated, contracts," whose main property seems to be the "unreadness" on the side of the nondrafter party. After all, it is a matter of fact that consumers are not prone to make the effort to read fine print, but often prefer signing after looking at some clauses only, such as price and other *salient* attributes.[5] Furthermore, the use of a boilerplate language implies that, even though consumers decide to read fine print, reading does not necessarily mean understanding. In other words, it is not given (rather, very unlikely) that an ordinary consumer is immediately able to understand clauses written in a technical legal language. For this reason, we say that reading fine print implies a cost on the side of consumers.[6]

Even assuming that consumers (or some of them) read and understand these clauses but do not totally agree with them, the drafter party usually refuses to replace,

[5] We will introduce the distinction between "salient" and "non salient" clauses in Chap. 3.

[6] For a more detailed analysis of reading costs see Sect. 1.4.2.

or simply to change, them. Since clauses are unalterable and consumers are only asked to agree to them, the only possible defense is to reject the whole contract. It is not surprising, however, that consumers may decide to accept even an obscure contract, especially when they have no alternative or when the cost of searching other alternatives is higher than the cost of accepting possibly unfavorable clauses. It is in light of these considerations that in the past some influential doctrine proposed, and for a certain time imposed, the idea that contracts of adhesion are more dangerous when the seller is a monopolist.[7] This view followed from the traditional economic thought that a free competitive market provides efficient clauses in equilibrium, especially if these clauses are those that consumers prefer. However, such theory can be true only when consumers are perfectly informed about any relevant aspect of the transaction they are involved in. This is an assumption that may collapse in the presence of contracts of adhesion if consumers have to pay a high cost to read some clauses or if they are not "sophisticated"[8] enough to take into account the risk involved in signing without reading.

1.2 Freedom of Contract (of Adhesion?) and Consumer Protection

The starting point of any general discussion about contract law cannot be anything but "freedom of contract." The principle affirms that, with the exception of some minimal regulation, parties must be free to bargain those clauses to include in their contracts without any government interference.

Economically thinking, freedom of contract corresponds to the theory of laissez-faire economics, which had an influential philosophical root in Locke's (1988) argument that society functions best when freely determined social contracts govern human behavior. In this sense, it can be said that in Locke's view freedom of contract becomes almost a natural right.

Maine (1861) expanded this idea declaring that

> (T)he movement of the progressive societies has hitherto been a movement from Status to Contract (p. 100).

A "status system" establishes obligations and relationships by birth, whereas a "contract system" presumes that the individuals are free and equal.

Modern Libertarianism, such as that represented by Nozick (1974), sees freedom of contract as the expression of a "minimal state," in which people pursue their interests by themselves only.

An economic evaluation of freedom of contract can be done in terms of efficiency. Using the Pareto-efficiency criterion, parties may reach an efficient

---

7 The presumptive influence of market structure on contract of adhesion performances will be presented and criticized in Sect. 1.3.1 and, in more details, in Chap. 2.

8 See Sect. 1.3.2.

allocation by trading those goods that constitute their initial endowments (or a single indivisible good for money) until none of them can be better off without making the others worse off.

Even the Coase theorem confirms that freedom of contract leads to an efficient solution. Coase (1960) argues that, any absent transaction cost and regardless of the legal allocation of rights, players would always be able to negotiate an efficient agreement.

In US, the Civil Rights Act of 1866 specifically listed the right "to make and enforce contracts" among the safeguarded liberties. The Constitution of United States protects freedom of contract in Article 1(10),

> No State shall enter into any Treaty, Alliance, or Confederation; grant Letters of Marque and Reprisal; coin Money; emit Bills of Credit; make any Thing but gold and silver Coin a Tender in Payment of Debts; pass any Bill of Attainder, ex post facto Law, or Law impairing the Obligation of Contracts, or grant any Title of Nobility.

This principle also inspired US doctrine and jurisprudence up to the introduction of Truman's New Deal in the 1930s when it started to be considered—as in the Supreme Court's main tendency—in favor of business rather than consumer welfare.

It was in the 1970s that freedom of contract was seriously criticized and constrained by new tendencies arising from the welfare state theory. Scholars have been so affected by this new tendency that Gilmore (1974) stated that contract freedom were dead.[9]

Absent from any law or courts' intervention, the enforcement of a contract follows the general provision that parties who have given their consent by signing the contract are bound to its content. Such a literal enforcement does not allow consumers to report their contract under the legal justification that they have a "duty to read" and are therefore presumed to have read and understood what they have signed. We will see in Chap. 5 how such rule inspired common law legislation in the past (and, in a less strict application, also in present times) as confirmation and protection of the freedom of contract principle. By contrast, the civil law approach has always been skeptical of the advantage of strictly defending freedom of contract without looking at specific circumstances that might deprive such principle of its proper purpose. According to this view, freedom of contract can be realized only if both parties can exercise it by giving their assent about a content they really know and accept.

It is in light of such considerations that both lawyers and economists argued about the importance of "a market for market information" (like advertising or price-comparison web-pages) that could realize efficiency without public intervention (like mandatory contract or quality disclosure). The basic idea is that high-quality firms have interest to disclose their contracts, so that consumers can infer that those nondisclosing sellers are offering low-quality goods. However, such remedy cannot

[9] On the same view, see also Atiyah (1979). On the opposed view, see the essays collected by Scheiber (1998) about common law tradition and interpretation.

be applied in concentrated markets where the presence of a few firms does not allow for comparisons. At the same time, it has a limited application even in competitive markets because it requires, on the one hand, responsible consumers who regularly undertake such market research[10]; and, on the other hand, responsible and independent intermediaries that rank firms using transparent criteria. However, the reason why we do not believe that the market for market information is a possible remedy to firm discretion in using fine print is that advertising and price-comparison websites usually use price as the main ranking criterion, while they usually offer no help in respect to other clauses such those written in fine print. Rather, price-comparison websites might even include disadvantageous fine print if they strengthen the focus on headline prices.

In presence of contracts of adhesion it seems that public intervention is the only possible remedy (see Sect. 1.7 and, in more details, Chap. 5). It implies that governments should (and very often do) intervene by law in order to deprive of force those clauses that have not been negotiated, establishing de facto that the drafter party has a "duty to speak": that is the duty of making the other party fully informed of the content of each clause. Despite the high value of this interpretation, its application is very expensive in practice. First of all, law should determine when and what contracts should not be enforced, since a general nonenforcement of any standard clause would turn out contract-destructive and incompatible with freedom of contract. We will see in Chap. 5 that legislative systems diverge across countries on this point: i.e., US laws usually leave to judges the evaluation of when and whether to intervene, whereas European law provides a detailed list of clauses that courts can or must overrule.

Generally speaking, the European tradition is much more inclined to that of the US to protect consumers by not enforcing nonnegotiated unfair clauses. In an intermediate position, the English system defends freedom of contract as general principle but, at the same time, is not reluctant to take into account specific situations that may require different rules, such as contracts of adhesion. In this sense, Lord Denning (1983) remarked that:

> None of you nowadays will remember the trouble we had - when I was called to the Bar - with exemption clauses. They were printed in small print on the back of tickets and order forms and invoices [...] He never read them or knew what was in them. No matter how unreasonable they were, he was bound. All this was done in the name of "freedom of contract."[...] No freedom for the little man who took the ticket or order form or invoice. The big concern said, "Take it or leave it." The little man had no option but to take it.[11]

Furthermore, overruling a clause requires its replacement with an external neutral and general standard. Since this standard has to fit the specific case under judgment, laws (or courts, when laws defer to them) usually replace unenforceable clauses with those that consumers would have accepted if they had read and fully

---

[10] As highlighted by Armstrong (2008), "while the market may provide market information, it cannot force consumers to undertake market research" (p. 109).

[11] George Mitchell (Chesterhall) Ltd v. Finney Lock Seeds Ltd [1983] QB 284, 297.

understood fine print. Such a rule is called "duty of good faith" and can be considered as a combination of the "duty to speak" and the "duty to read."

In the nineteenth and in the early twentieth century, the traditional doctrine[12] was quite reluctant to recognize a specific discipline for contracts of adhesion different from the main contract law. In particular, to support the enforceability of standard form contracts such doctrine started from the assumption that the nondrafter's signature on a document must be treated as an assent to every clause the document contains.[13] In this sense, it is irrelevant whether the adherent actually read and understood it. Exceptions of such rules were found in traditional cases that determined whatever contract unenforceable (such as fraud, unilateral or mutual mistake, incapacity given by age or mental conditions, and/or duress). Fraud refers to any situation in which a party intentionally makes the other party not informed of the contract content, while unilateral mistake concerns those situations in which, absent from fraud, one party has a misrepresentation of the contract that the other party could have avoided. By contrast, when misrepresentation cannot be avoided and cannot be referred to the other party, the contract is unenforceable because of a mutual mistake,[14] usually invoked whenever it cannot be possible to prove fraud or unilateral mistake.[15] Likewise, law cannot allow for contract enforceability when one party's assent has been given under coercion or duress, as the case in which someone signs the contract at gunpoint: the reason is that no assent has been given as no alternative was in fact available.

This doctrinal view changed from the second half of twentieth century when lawyers started thinking that some limitations to freedom of contract, different from the traditional ones mentioned above, were necessary in the presence of contracts of adhesion.[16]

Economically, the main reason to limit freedom of contract concerns the existence of any situation that cannot allow for efficiency. Traditional examples in this sense are market failures, like asymmetric information, transaction costs, or distributional purposes. Turning back to the Pareto-efficiency concept, free trade leads to an efficient outcome only if markets function correctly without externalities or informational asymmetries. On this point, Ben-Shahar (2009) argues that in terms of a cost–benefit analysis, a duty to read regime could be the right solution whenever the cost of reading a text is not too high[17]; vice versa, when such cost becomes high in respect to the benefit, then reading is not an efficient choice and a

---

[12] See Wigmore (1981).

[13] See Upton v. Tribilcock, 91 U.S. 45. 50 (1875), Hoshaw v. Cosgriff, 247 F 22. 26 (1917), Morstad v. Atchison. T & S.F. Ry., 23 N.M. 663, 160 P. 886 (1918), G.L. Webster Co. v. Trinidad NBean & Elevator Co., 92 F.2d 177 (1937).

[14] See Posner and Rosenfield (1977) and Ayres and Rasmusen (1993).

[15] See Chirelstein (2006).

[16] Such a different view was also included in the Restatement (Second) of Contract, section 211 (3), 1979. For a deep discussion about the Draft of the Restatement, see Dawson (1976).

[17] Ben-Shahar (2005) made the example of the "black box" warning for a drug where the text is reasonably short and easy to read.

consumer cannot be considered liable for not having made an inefficient (because too expensive) activity. Furthermore, even if efficient, it is not given that such an outcome is also fair.

These arguments arise strong evidence based on both fairness and efficiency considerations to sustain the need of some regulation to limit freedom of contract in the presence of contracts of adhesion.

It is interesting now to make a comparative analysis of what lawyers and economists, respectively, invoke as main arguments to limit freedom of contract. We analyze the law literature in next section; then we will turn to the economic literature in Sects. 1.4 and 1.5, focusing on the transaction costs related to the presence of unilaterally drafted fine print, with particular attention devoted to reading costs.

1.3 The Traditional Legal Reasons to Protect Consumers

In this section, we analyze the doctrine of unconscionability that lawyers have used in order to limit the application of freedom of contract. In contract law, a contract is defined unconscionable when it is unfair or extremely one-sided in favor of the party who has the superior bargaining power. An unconscionable contract can be defined as an agreement that mentally competent people would not enter into and that no fair and honest person would accept. It is for that reason that unconscionable contracts usually result from exploiting consumers who are often poorly educated in legal subtleties.

As a result, according to the theory of unconscionability, since consumers cannot negotiate contract clauses and are not used to read clauses at all, the fact that they sign the contract does not prove their meaningful consent to all its clauses.[18] For this reason, courts should refuse to enforce one-sided standard clauses literally, but rather should interpret them *contra proferentem* in the logic of what consumers could have *reasonably* expected from those clauses.

The main factors used to support the unconscionability and the related doctrines of reasonable expectations are now analyzed in details.

The first traditional factor is not related to parties, but rather looks at the market in which trade takes place. In particular, in the past there was an influential doctrinal tendency, also confirmed by courts, of not enforcing one-sided clauses whenever the seller exploited a market power.

The second factor is person-sensitive and refers to parties' incapacity of understanding the contract content. It leads to lack of sophistication and contract complexity.

[18] On this point, Llewelling (1960) defined consumers' consent to the boilerplate included in standard form contract as a "blank" consent.

To define the notion of lack of sophistication, lawyers usually distinguish between "consumer contracts" and "B2B contracts." "Consumer contracts" are those contracts in which the nondrafter party is not involved in a job transaction and is presumed not to have enough knowledge to read and understand every clause included into the contract. B2B contracts are those in which both parties are "professional" and therefore fully informed of any aspect of the transaction they are involved into. We will refer to a different version of sophistication, focusing on consumers' rationality (see Sect. 1.3.2).

The third factor refers to the contract structure. Since contracts are unilaterally drafted by the seller and nonnegotiated, the main source of consumers' incapacity is certainly the usage of fine print and, more generally, a technical language that turns out very hard to read and to understand even for attentive consumers.

1.3.1 Market Power

In economic terms, it is well known that inefficiency characterizing any noncompetitive market, above all a monopoly, is due to the combination of the seller's market power with asymmetric information. As underlined by Hermalin et al. (2006), it is a matter of screening. If the monopolist were able to perfectly price discriminate, he could satisfy the whole market demand charging a personalized price equal to the reservation price for each consumer. Thus, the monopolist would get the entire market surplus, but the outcome would turn out efficient because the social welfare would be maximized. Unfortunately (or fortunately), to do so the monopolist should be able to know the reservation price for each consumer, that is obviously impossible.

However, the risk involved in the seller's market power is not only an increase in price. It is also a matter of bargaining power. In other words, a nondiscriminating monopolist can propose the consumer a take-it-or-leave-it offer at his own conditions. By doing so, the monopolist can exploit clauses different from price, which are unfavorable to consumers, but make the monopolist's expected costs decrease.

According to these preliminary considerations, lawyers have stressed that regulation is necessary whenever the seller can exploit such bargaining power against consumers, and therefore whenever he exploits a market power.

This view is supported by the traditional economic theory saying that competition between sellers will push the market to the efficient equilibrium.

According to the economic theory, on the one hand it is relatively easy to justify the presence of standard clauses when the drafter exploits some market power as long as these clauses turn out in his own interest, although inefficient on a social point of view. On the other hand, it is rather problematic to harmonize inefficient standard clauses with the logic of competition.

Clearly, there are two possible explanations: either every market characterized by the usage of standard clauses is in some way monopolistic (or at least, it cannot be considered truly competitive) or whenever a market is competitive contract clauses must be efficient even if standard.

However, both solutions collapse on an empirical point of view because it is a matter of fact that even competitive markets, where competitiveness refers to the absence of entry or exit barriers, are not saved from the usage of contracts of adhesion (see Marotta-Wurgler 2008). At the same time, it is again a matter of fact that some of these standard clauses usually serve the seller/drafter's interests and turn out socially inefficient.

It raises an important question, whether the presence of many enough sellers/ retailers into a market is a sufficient condition to assert that a market is competitive.

We claim that whenever consumers have to bear a cost to understand every clause (including those in fine print), competition between sellers cannot work properly. To see this, think that competing in clauses is costly for sellers, e.g., offering a full warranty increases seller's costs more than offering a partial warranty or not offering any warranty. Trivially, the seller's potential gain from offering high-quality clauses is to increase his sales to the detriment of competitors. However, this incentive might be overtaken by the likely risk that consumers do not read every clause and cannot appreciate the difference among different contracts. These considerations seem to rely on the presence of nonsophisticated consumers (see next subsection), who do not understand the risk involved in fine print. We rather claim that the same sort of arguments works even assuming that consumers are all smart enough to understand the presence of fine print and the potential danger of signing the contract without reading.

In next chapter, we will provide a more detailed analysis of the literature focusing on the unequal bargaining power between parties, starting from the "market structure hypothesis" and then turning to the critics moved on both theoretical and empirical sides.

1.3.2 Lack of Sophistication

There is a general agreement among lawyers that a strict duty to read cannot apply to "consumer contracts," usually drafted by the seller. The explanation evoked to support this thesis is that on average consumers are not sophisticated enough. What said requires a clarification of what lawyers refer to as "sophistication" or "sophisticated parties," since it differs from its economic meaning.

From a lawyers' point of view an economic agent is sophisticated when she has sufficient technical knowledge to understand the meaning of what she is doing (in this case, the content of the contract she is signing). Then, when lawyers refer to contracts between sophisticated parties, they usually refer to those contracts among "professionals" (called B2B contracts) in which the nondrafting party is also involved in a job transaction. In this sense, "sophistication" refers to an individual's technical skills as a consequence of her profession.

By contrast, as developed in more details in Chap. 3, "sophistication" in economics means "rationality": an individual is sophisticated if she makes her choice after having taken into account any possible *available* information and, at the same time, the eventual existence of any *non-available* information. Accordingly, those consumers who are not able to understand what is written fine print without paying a reading cost are sophisticated as long as they take into account the risk involved in signing without reading.

In this sense, the economic concept of sophistication as rationality diverges from its legal meaning concerning the individual's capacity (given by age, mental conditions and so on) of being aware of what he is doing and, in our specific context, of being party of a contract. When lawyers say that the nondrafting party is not sophisticated they do not mean that consumers are irrational, but simply that they cannot be fully informed of the content of the contract without reading or that they do not possess enough skills to read and understand the contract without legal assistance.

Rather, arguing that consumers are not sophisticated in economics means that they are not fully rational. For example, they ignore freely available information that might be relevant to a further decision (see again Chap. 3).

Nevertheless, lawyers and economists agree that in all these contexts some regulation may be necessary as it turns out fair and efficient at the same time. The problem then becomes when and how to intervene.

Lawyers usually agree to apply a strict duty to read in B2B contracts in which both parties are legally sophisticated where the use of standard form contracts may turn out even useful also to the nondrafting party.[19] In this sense, Ahdieh (2006) showed that standard form contracts can signal

> the absence of any undisclosed reason for standard form contracts to be less attractive to the relevant party (p. 1043).

Using Schelling's (1960) language, standard form contracts may thus work as "focal point" in transactions among sophisticated parties since a favorable deviation from standard form contracts may work as an adverse signal and may raise the question "Why?" in consumers' minds.

Hill and King (2004) argued that it might be expensive for a party to convince the other party that deviating from standard form contracts can be favorable for both of them. Bernstein (1993) termed these costs as "relational costs" and suggested that a proposal of a contract different from an accepted default clause might be seen as a signal that the drafting party is litigious and tends to rely on legal rights.

As a logical consequence of this approach, it follows that when parties are sophisticated there is no reason for not enforcing standard clauses. As such, a traditional "duty to read" rule can apply.[20] It allows a distinction between a general

---

[19] The German doctrine is an exception: the safeguard offered by the German Standard Clauses Statute applies to every contract; while the EU Directive applies to consumer contracts only.

[20] Under a "duty to read" rule the contract is enforceable irrespective of consumers' awareness on its content.

"competition policy" that aims to remove any barrier for a competitive market to work, and a specific "consumer policy" that consists of protecting consumers because of their "weakness" in respect to the drafter party.[21]

In order to analyze the contract unbalance between the two parties where the seller drafts the contract and is therefore "stronger" than the consumer, we will focus on consumer contracts and we will use the notion of sophistication in its economic meaning. Accordingly, even not professional, a consumer is sophisticated as long as she takes into account the risk involved in signing a contract of adhesion without reading fine print. At the same time, since she is not professional, even if sophisticated, a consumer cannot understand the content of some clauses without reading them at a certain cost.

Vice versa, we call naïve consumers those consumers who do not take into account the risk involved in signing a contract of adhesion without reading fine print.

We will claim that the too much emphasis has been made in the literature to consumers' lack of sophistication since it may play an active role only if the proportion of naïve consumers is large enough. Chapter 3 will provide a more detailed analysis of consumer naïvity and its effect on the equilibrium outcome.

1.3.3 Contract Complexity

The theory about market power leads directly to the theory of contract complexity.

We have seen that the unconscionability test has been the main doctrinal expedient used by courts in order to override some unfair clauses. A claim of unconscionability cannot be determined merely by examining the face of the contract; rather, there must be an inquiry into the circumstances under which the contract was executed, its purpose, and effects. In the courts' viewpoint, unconscionability must present two different components: a procedural component and a substantive component.

The procedural component is satisfied by the existence of hidden clauses, frequent in the context of contracts of adhesion. In this sense, it concerns how clauses have been included into the contract (such as in the use of boilerplate language), the consumer's reasonable ignorance of the existence of some clauses in the contract (usually called "unfair surprise"), and more generally the adhesive nature of the contract itself. In the courts' viewpoint, the condition is satisfied whenever the nondrafter party has no negotiation role, but can simply accept or reject the offer.

The substantive component concerns the clause content itself and is satisfied when it appears so one-sided to be oppressive.[22] An example of this is the inclusion

---

[21] See Armstrong (2008).

[22] There are several decisions defining the concept of substantive unconscionability, such as Rosenberg, 170 F.3d at 17, Armendariz, 6 P3d at 690, Harris, 183 F3d at 181.

of an arbitration clause requiring that any legal dispute proposed by the consumer about any aspect of the contract must be devolved to private arbitration rather than to a public jury. Such clauses turn out onerous for consumers since private arbitration is very expensive, and may restrict them in asserting their right. Other examples of clauses usually declared unenforceable as a result of their unreasonableness are those that allocate the risk of some loss to the party less able to prevent it.

Roughly speaking, the European legal tradition has been more inclined than that of the US to use the unconscionability test. The first US scholar who addressed such a problem in standard form contracts was Llewellyn (1960) who wrote that

> [I]nstead of thinking about 'assent' to boilerplate clauses, we can recognize that so far as concerns the specific, there is no assent at all (p. 362).

Since a contract binds parties even in the presence of standard form contracts, Llewellyn proposed to qualify as "blanket" the agreement given by the nondrafter to a nonread contract.[23] Stressing the substantive notion of unconscionability rather than the procedural element, he affirmed that the nondrafter were bound in face of his signature "to any not unreasonable or indecent clause" (p. 363), providing a legitimate foundation of not enforcing unfair clauses.

Chapter 4 will focus on sellers' incentive to make the contract *conscionable*. We therefore see whether sellers have an interest to voluntarily disclose fine print, and whether market structure matters in this sense. We also provide an analysis focusing on the effects of disclosure on consumers' welfare to show that they do not necessarily gain from disclosure.

1.4 When Price Is Not the Only Cost for Consumers

Consumers are used to look at price as the main cost of the transaction. Attentive consumers may care of other accessory costs, as shipping costs, warranty extension costs, potential litigation costs and so on. All these costs, however, correspond to a specific service the consumer receives.

In addition, contracts of adhesion impose other costs to consumers that do not correspond to specific goods or services, but are simply instrumental to the transaction.[24] The higher these costs, the less efficient the transaction.

In this subsection, we will analyze these hidden costs, starting from searching costs and then moving to the most important case of reading costs.

---

[23] Similarly, White (2000) defines the assent given to clauses which consumers are not used to read as "autistic."

[24] About the interpretation of reading costs as transaction costs see Sovern (2006).

1.4.1 Searching Costs

In general terms, this work is related to the literature focusing on the role of consumers' uncertainty on their purchasing decisions. First of all, there is a large amount of literature exploring the effects of consumers' searching costs on the equilibrium outcome. One of the most important results in this field is the so-called Diamond's paradox.

Diamond (1971) showed that the existence of even small searching costs will lead to equilibrium prices in a competitive market from the Bertrand solution up to the monopoly level. The intuition behind the Diamond's paradox is quite simple. He considered a competitive market with price-setting firms that produce a homogeneous product. Absent from any capacity constraints, a small price cut would capture all sales if it can be freely observed by consumers, so that sellers would cut their own price to the marginal cost in the Bertrand equilibrium. Diamond showed that equilibrium outcome changes significantly when prices cannot be freely observed, but consumers search sequentially for price information and must pay a search cost in order to observe a given seller's price.

He presented a sequential model of several periods of time. Each period firms simultaneously set prices and each consumer can enter one shop only. Consumers observe the price for free in the first period and can decide to buy or to leave the shop (thinking that the price is too high) in order to enter another the following period at a given positive cost. Firms know consumers' demand and in particular consumers' reservation price[25]; while consumers know just the distribution of prices, and have to compare the search cost they face in order to enter another shop with the expected gain of finding a lower price.

Given these conditions, no equilibrium exists in which sellers set nonmonopoly prices. The intuition is quite straightforward: a sufficiently small increase in price made by one seller will not alter the probability that a consumer will pay to observe that price, and furthermore will not represent a sufficient incentive for consumers to pay another search cost to get an alternative price offer. Sellers have unilateral incentives to raise price and these incentives exist as long as price is below monopoly levels. When the number of firms is large enough, then there exists an equilibrium in which all firms set monopoly prices. The paradox of this model is that its argument does not depend on the magnitude of the search cost, as long as it is positive; rather, when searching costs are zero, then the equilibrium price falls discontinuously down to the Bertrand level.

The Diamond's paradox had a strong impact on the literature and other authors have studied the topic looking for some possible extensions. Wolinsky (1986) showed that the Diamond's paradox does not apply if there is some degree of product heterogeneity because consumers are induced to search even if prices are

[25] The Diamond's paradox would still hold if sellers knew just the distribution of reservation prices throughout the population.

the same. As consequence, price tends to decrease approximately to the competitive level.

Holt and Davis (1995) found an empirical confirmation of Diamond's theoretical result by running a six-session experiment consisting of two treatments. In the "Posted Price" treatment, consumers observe prices before paying the search or travel cost. Conversely, in the "Search" treatment consumers have to pay the search cost (15 cents) in order to know the price. Results confirm the Diamond's paradox. After a preliminary adjustment, prices fall down to the competitive equilibrium in of each session of the "Posted Price" treatment, whereas they remain constant between the competitive and the monopoly levels in the "Search" treatment.

Several authors have also tried to solve the Diamond's paradox. Bagwell and Ramey (1992) introduced a "loyalty-boycott search rule" in the model that allows consumers to boycott sellers who raise price by going to their rivals in future searches and to be loyal to those sellers who do not raise price. Such a model fits quite well those markets characterized by frequent low-cost transactions, like groceries, restaurants, etc.

Fershtman and Fishman (1989) suggested another solution showing that the Diamond's paradox does not hold if the sequential search technology is replaced by a noisy search technology as noise approaches zero.

Other authors proposed different dynamic-price settings: von zur Muehlen (1980), Rob (1985) and Stiglitz (1985) set up their models in order to obtain price dispersion in equilibrium under an optimal but static price-setting rule, while Bénabou (1988) set up a dynamic model of monopolistic competition in an inflationary environment with sequential search, price dynamics, and free entry on both sides of consumers and sellers. He showed that inflation determines price dispersion and it makes search potentially profitable, thereby favoring competition. More particularly, when price dispersion increases (so that also inflation increases) high searching costs will lead to higher equilibrium prices and determine an increase in price dispersion. It allows price to fluctuate in equilibrium from the Bertrand level to the Diamond level depending on search cost levels.

1.4.2 Reading Costs

In the context of contracts of adhesion, consumers usually face a cost not in order to know the price, but in order to know other contract clauses different from price. We have already highlighted that these clauses are hidden in fine print and written in complex legal language, so that reading these clauses turns out costly to consumers, and possibly frustrating and even pointless. Using Ben-Shahar's (2008) suggestive words:

> And what if they did read? Surely, there is nothing they can do about the bad stuff they know they will find. Are they going to cross out the unfavorable clause? Are they going to call some semi-automatic 'customer service agent' and negotiate? Other than lose the excitement about the deal and maybe walk away from it (to what? A better contract?), there

> is not much individuals can do. Dedicated readers can expect only heartache, which is a very poor reward for engaging in such time-consuming endeveor. Apart from an exotic individual here or there, nobody reads (p. 2).

Despite of these considerations, it is still true that reading is an opportunity, even though costly, even though not always implemented. Saying that consumers manifest assent to the contract simply because they actually had the opportunity to read is probably controversial, but certainly the opportunity to read, even though at some cost, produces important effects on the final outcome.

Precisely, reading costs affect the final equilibrium price less strongly than searching costs in Diamond. In particular, using a simple formal model (see the Appendix), we will see that the reading cost may keep price above the Bertrand level but below the monopoly level in an unregulated competitive market. It follows from the fact that, contrary to Diamond, as long as consumers can observe price for free in every contract of adhesion, sellers cannot increase their prices to the monopoly level. The intuition is the following:

1. Consumers would find it unprofitable to read clauses if they are charged the monopoly price;
2. No seller would therefore include friendly clauses if consumers did not read;
3. Consumers would not buy at any price higher than their reservation level for an unfriendly contract;
4. Competition will lead sellers to reduce price down to the Bertrand level.

However, if price is higher than the production cost but below a given threshold, consumers may decide to invest in reading with some positive probability and sellers may find it profitable to include friendly clauses with some positive probability.

Clearly, the presence of a positive reading cost gives an information advantage to the drafter party, the seller(s). Thus, as well shown in the literature on asymmetric information, it is not surprising that the final outcome turns out inefficient. The market for lemons by Akerlof's (1970) is probably the most famous example in this field. In Akerlof's model, rational consumers have to decide whether to buy an used car after observing only the price, so that they use it as signal to make inference about the unknown car quality level. The model proves that under asymmetric information trade between parties may not occur in equilibrium because price works as a signal of quality for consumers. As the price goes down, the expected quality decreases and consumers' expected utility becomes negative. It makes trade unfeasible even for very low levels of price.

Unlike Akerlof, trade is feasible when asymmetric information refers to contract clauses: the reason is that consumers have the chance of being fully informed of contract clauses by reading them at some positive cost. Nevertheless, the outcome is inefficient because to do so they have to pay a wasteful reading cost.

The economic literature related to the concept of reading costs focused on its effects on consumers' choice between accepting or rejecting a contract of adhesion.

A preliminary conclusion is that consumers usually do not read clauses written in fine print (Marotta-Wurgler 2008).

1.5 When Production Costs Are Not the Only Cost for Sellers

Turning to the production side, there are some additional costs for sellers different from the cost of producing the good of a given quality level. We will focus on the cost of writing the contract and on the cost of disclosing fine print which sellers may decide to bear in order to make their contracts transparent and freely readable.

1.5.1 Writing (or Printing) Costs

As unilaterally drafted and preprinted, a contract of adhesion implies a writing cost. The role of writing costs is unanimously considered rather unimportant relative to reading costs. The reason is that (as carefully underlined by Rasmusen 2001) the usage of boilerplate language makes writing costs very small because the same clause will be reproduced in each contract. From an economic viewpoint, there are scale economies that characterize sellers' production of contract clauses. In this sense, boilerplate can be intended as a "public good"[26] for drafter parties since the same clause can be included without any additional cost in any contract proposed to any potential consumer. As a logical consequence, it implies that the so-called writing cost endured by the drafter party is very small, almost irrelevant, in comparison with the reading cost endured by the nondrafter party, and roughly corresponds to the cost of printing several pages of terms and conditions.

1.5.2 Disclosing (or Speaking) Costs

Obviously, sellers are not constrained to include fine print in their contract. That is, they are free to disclose clauses, e.g. by writing them in plain and clear language.

Disclosing costs are essentially fixed: they do not vary with the number of customers (and therefore the frequency of disclosures) and do not depend on the nature of the good/service on sale or on the size of the firm. This turns out in favor of the disclosing seller: since he may not need to raise the price in order to cover

---

[26] See again Ben-Shahar (2009). See also Davis (2006), who analyzed the boilerplate use in nonprofit organizations, and Choi and Gulati (2006), who analyzed a seller's incentives of using boilerplate.

these costs he does not lose in competitiveness. In turn, we would expect competitive sellers to be pushed to disclose their clauses hurting potentially entrant firms.

Disclosing (or speaking) costs matter in Katz (1990) and must be taken into account in order to choose among interpretation rules. Katz developed a bargaining model in a form-contract setting involving a seller and a consumer, both drawn from a population of sellers and consumers of various types. Types are given by individual's preferences over quality that is private information on the side of the seller.

The contract offered is a pair (p, z) where p is price (the salient attribute) and $z \in [0,1]$ is the seller's proposal for the value of quality. It means that, depending on the legal rule enforced, the seller might offer a value of z different from the true quality level.

The seller is allowed to offer an explicit contract by paying a speaking cost that allows the consumer to observe both clauses without cost. As an alternative, the seller can offer a form contract which allows the consumer to observe just the price for free, but requires her to pay a reading cost in order to know the value of z. If offered an explicit contract, the consumer has to decide whether to buy or not the good. If offered a form contract, the consumer must also decide whether to read it or not.

Katz modeled some interpretation rule such that the lowest (highest) possible quality level that the seller can offer when it speaks is lower (higher) than the lowest (highest) possible quality level that he can offer when silent.

It means that under a strict duty to speak, the seller is free to choose the level of quality he prefers. If some mandatory quality is provided, then the choice about z collapses to a single point. Accordingly, if the seller decides to speak without any legal limit or rule, he will choose the level of quality that maximizes its expected profits. In the presence of some limits imposed by law, a speaking seller will choose the profit maximizing quality level if compatible with them, otherwise it will choose the closest possible admitted level, earning the profit associated with that level minus the speaking cost. On the other hand, if the seller decides to remain silent and chooses z according to the corresponding limits, then the consumer forms her expectation about quality given the observed price and chooses whether to read and, if not, whether to accept or to reject the offer.

Katz showed that if the speaking cost is sufficiently high, there is no difference between a strict duty to read and a strict duty to speak, both imposing the same minimum quality level. Again, there is neither difference between a strict duty to read with an absolute minimum quality level and a mandatory rule that imposes to the seller the same minimum quality level. These results follow from the assumption that a speaking seller makes reading free for consumers (that is reading costs collapse to zero).

In the following analysis, we will allow sellers to disclose their clauses at some cost (see Chap. 4), and we will assume that the disclosing cost is cheaper than the reading cost.

1.6 Public Intervention

Generally speaking, there is a large consensus that every legal system must protect consumers against evidently unfair, nonnegotiated clauses: the key question in examining different legal systems is how protective these measures should be. In the last chapter, we will compare the US and European systems to see that they indeed present strong differences in the protection offered to consumers, in the sense that European laws propose a regulation on clauses, whereas the US laws have opted for a regulation on disclosure. What these systems have in common is the important role played by courts in identifying high-risk cases.

The main court tendency in the US system is to interpret any unfair clause such that consumers would have accepted it if fully informed of its content. Another policy, similar to the EU system, consists in laws banning some clauses as unfair and requiring some others as mandatory. Both policies obviously carry on a cost for consumers[27] in order to turn to a court. It implies that, to be effective, mandatory clauses require monitoring systems, as those implemented by the European Commission, to ascertain that sellers respect new rules; in regard to the courts' intervention, as in the US system, it requires easy access for consumers to courts by consumer associations and class actions.

Such policies are slightly different from what Katz (1990) refers to as "duty to speak" rules. Saying that the courts interpret any contract clause in favor of consumers does not mean that sellers must disclose (according to Katz's terminology, they must *speak*). The same argument applies to mandatory clauses. It is an important argument which allows to say that whatever policy is implemented it makes disclosing costs equal to 0.

Such conclusion is justified in light of the fact that sellers have not to make their contract easy to read because public intervention works as a warranty of friendly terms. After all, forcing sellers to disclose would not sort out any effect if the disclosing cost were so high that they will prefer not to trade.

Furthermore, we claim that even if regulation focusing on hidden clauses turns out efficient, it is not given that it will be also consumer protective, if not accompanied by a regulation on price. This effect is emphasized in concentrated markets if most consumers are sophisticated.

1.7 The Game Theoretical Approach

At the end of each chapter, we propose an Appendix that formally proves the main arguments proposed therein.

[27] It may be the case in which mandatory rules are imposed by some agencies able to underwrite consumers' costs or can defend consumers at trials.

Since a contract is a legal phenomenon involving at least two parties, it is relatively easy to model the transaction as a formal game able to provide an intuition of what parties are expected to do in equilibrium and whether the equilibrium/equilibria is/are efficient.

Game theory is the science of strategy. Each player chooses the action among the available strategies that maximizes his (expected) payoffs given the other players' strategies. Players, strategies, and payoffs are the main elements of the game and are determined by the law of the game.

In the case of standard form contracts, the law of the game imposes a transaction eventually to take place without negotiation between players, identified as sellers and consumers. The game is played in sequence. In round 1, sellers offer a pre-printed contract and decide the price to charge and whether to include some clauses in fine print; in round 2 consumers observe the price and decide whether to read fine print or whether to accept or reject the offer without reading.

Players' payoffs are determined by the opposite preferences on price and clause quality: the seller's (consumer's) payoff increases (decreases) in price and decreases (increases) in clause quality.

Since sellers draft the contract without consumers' participation, they are obviously more informed about the contract clauses and may exploit this informational power in order to raise their payoffs to the detriment of consumers. We allow consumers to fill the informational gap by reading fine print; however, reading is costly and consumers have to decide whether to read or not to read by forming (rational) beliefs about what sellers might have included in fine print.

For the sake of simplicity, suppose that clauses can turn out either friendly or unfriendly to consumers. Since the game is characterized by asymmetric information and is played sequentially, it will be solved looking for Perfect Bayesian Equilibria (PBE) in pure and mixed strategies. Every equilibrium can be intended as a solution of the game since it is such that no player can profitably deviate. A PBE is a strategy profile and a belief system such that the strategies are sequentially rational given the belief system and the belief system is *consistent* given the strategy profile. If each player believes that the other player will implement only a strategy in equilibrium, then that equilibrium is in pure strategies. Conversely, if at least one player believes that the other player will mix between two or more strategies in equilibrium, then that equilibrium is in mixed strategies. Mixed strategy equilibria arises when the player who mixes, e.g., between two strategies gets exactly the same (expected) payoff from each of them, and is therefore indifferent. Then, suppose that he tosses a hypothetical coin and decides the strategy to implement accordingly.

If consumers believe that sellers always offer friendly clauses, they will never read them in order to economize on the related cost, and will always accept the contract; however, if consumers never read fine print, then sellers have a profitable deviation to including unfriendly cheap clauses. Then, given the strategy profile, consumer beliefs turn out inconsistent and cannot be supported in equilibrium.

Similarly, consumers will not read even if they believe that sellers have included unfriendly terms in fine print, and will accept the offer only if price is not higher than their reservation level for an unfriendly contract.

It implies that reading will take place in equilibrium only if consumers' (sellers') beliefs that the contract contains friendly clauses (that consumers read) in probabilistic terms are greater than 0 but less than 1, and both sellers and consumers will behave accordingly.

Beliefs are formed rationally if players are rational. We will see that naïve consumers hold priori beliefs, e.g., they believe that obscure clauses are always friendly. In this case, we say that beliefs are exogenous and do not enter the equilibrium concept since they have not to be consistent with the strategy profile. Since naïve beliefs do not vary with price and clause quality, naïve consumers are even weaker then sophisticated consumers. Precisely, both categories are less informed than sellers about the content of fine print, but sophisticated consumers are able to defend themselves and discipline the sellers, even when they do not read, using skeptical out-of-equilibrium beliefs about a given seller's deviation from a putative equilibrium. To clarify this last point, consider a monopoly and suppose that an equilibrium prescribes that the monopolist offers an unfriendly contract charging a price equal to consumers' reservation level for that contract (call this level x^*) To be an equilibrium it must be that no player has a profitable deviation. Suppose that the monopolist deviates to a friendly contract charging more than x^*. If consumers are rational they have to form beliefs about every deviating contract that, by definition, arises out-of-the equilibrium path. If consumers believe that every such contract is unfriendly they will reject the deviating contract, and such a deviation will turn out not profitable to the monopolist. We refer to this formation process of out-of-equilibrium beliefs as "adverse inference." Suppose per contra that consumers believe that a deviating contract is friendly. This example explains how adverse beliefs protect unaware consumers from sellers' exploitation.

We will use game theory in order to prove formally that the main factors constituting the unconscionability doctrine are not exhaustive in order to decide when and how laws or courts should intervene.

In next chapter, we will start from a basic model in which consumers are all sophisticated and sellers cannot disclose their terms. We will compare the outcome across opposite market structures, a monopoly and a competitive market. Our results reject the market structure hypothesis, proving that both markets are characterized by inefficient one-sided fine print.

In Chap. 3, we will relax the assumption on consumer's rationality and will introduce naïve consumers in order to understand whether and how their presence affects sellers' strategy across markets. Although consumers' lack of sophistication has been emphasized in the literature as the main reason of inefficiency, our results mitigate this approach, showing that naïve consumers are able to influence the equilibrium outcome only if they are a large percentage.

In Chap. 4, will allow sellers to disclose their contracts at some positive cost to see who eventually gains from contract disclosure. We will prove that sophisticated consumers usually do not gain from disclosure, especially when they face a monopolist.

Finally, in Chap. 5, we will analyze the effects of some regulation on the equilibrium outcome. We will see that regulations focusing on hidden and unconscionable clauses does not turn out consumer protective, but risks to harm sophisticated consumers and to favor the monopolist if not accompanied by a regulation on price and/or other *conscionable* clauses.

Each chapter, including the present one, ends with an Appendix where we propose a simple game theoretical model formally proving our main results.

Appendix

In this Appendix, we sketch the game theoretical model we will use throughout the manuscript.

Consider the market for a certain good produced by $N \geq 1$ identical sellers (S) and a unit mass of identical rational consumers (B). In particular, $N = 1$ in a monopoly, whereas N is finite and very large in a competitive market.

Sellers produce a good that looks like identical to consumers, but may vary in the quality of clauses included into the contract according to $q = \{l, h\}$, with $h > l$. As an example, suppose that the seller can offer a warranty against possible damages: whether the warranty is friendly or not to consumers depends on clauses and conditions regulating its extension and limits. Thus, if a warranty is formally offered but clauses and conditions are so strict to make it substantially impossible to come in use, the clause turns out unfriendly alike to no warranty being given. Accordingly, we refer to high-quality clauses as those turning out consumer-friendly, and to low-quality clauses as those turning out consumer unfriendly. Clause quality is endogenous as each seller decides what kind of clauses to include in his contract. Without loss of generality, we assume that sellers face no cost if they offer unfriendly clauses, and pay $c > 0$ to insert friendly clauses.

Consumers get a utility equal to 0 when they do not buy and a utility $u(q)$ once they buy the good. Call $u_l = u(q_l)$ and $u_h = u(q_h)$ with $u_h > u_l > 0$.[28]

Sellers simultaneously draft contracts. Each contract contains up to two clauses. The first is price p, whereas the second one is included in fine print[29] and can be either friendly or unfriendly, depending on whether it includes, e.g., a warranty or not. The same analysis can be conducted assuming that the contract contains more than two clauses. We have made the model as simple as possible since contract complexity would not change our results as consumers would infer the content of additional clauses by looking at the number of clauses included in equilibrium.

---

[28] Trivially, no transaction would be feasible if $u_h < 0$.

[29] This assumption will be relaxed in Chap. 4 when we will allow sellers to voluntarily disclose their contracts.

We do not include any writing cost in the analysis because, according to the literature, it is usually small and insignificant.[30]

Once a seller decides the nature of the contract clauses, the contract is offered to all potential consumers. The seller(s) have no interest to discriminate as long as all consumers are rational and share the same preferences on quality. It is an assumption that will be relaxed in Chap. 3 when we will introduce naïve consumers. However, even under those circumstances, sellers must offer the same contract to every consumer. Then seller(s)' payoff per customer is given by p per unit sold if no warranty is offered and by $p - c$ otherwise.

Consumers observe price without any cost, but they must pay a reading cost $k \geq 0$ in order to read and to understand whether the second clause is friendly or unfriendly.[31] Consumers who reject earn 0 if they decide not to read and $-k$ otherwise. Consumers who accept without reading earn $u_h - p$ if clauses are friendly, and $u_l - p$ otherwise. Consumers who accept after reading earn k less in each eventuality.

For the sake of simplicity, we assume that the game is played only once: in other words the model does not allow for resampling. Nevertheless, most of our results would survive otherwise.

Consumers cannot negotiate any contract clause even when they read. It implies that seller(s) can only offer contracts of adhesion. We will use a condition, thereafter referred to as *Efficiency Condition*:

$$u_h - c - k > u_l > 0$$

The left-hand side inequality means that efficiency is maximized if sellers offer friendly clauses; the right-hand side inequality means that trading with unfriendly clauses is more efficient than no trade.

We will solve the game by searching for symmetric perfect Bayesian equilibria (from now on, simply defined as *equilibria*) in pure and mixed strategies in both a monopoly and a competitive market.

---

[30] It may consists on writing/printing costs: see Sect. 1.5.1.

[31] We will allow sellers to make clauses fully transparent in Chap. 4.

Chapter 2
Market Structure

2.1 The "Market Structure Hypothesis"

One of the main theorists of the unequal bargaining power theory was Kessler (1943), who argued that the risk of unfair clauses (corresponding to unfriendly clauses in our simple model) is very high especially in those markets in which sellers have market power, above all in the case of a monopoly. By contrast, competition among several firms should lead them to provide efficient clauses at the lowest possible price.

In Kessler's view,

> [T]he law, by protecting the unequal distribution of property, does nothing to prevent freedom of contract from becoming a one-sided privilege [...] Standard contracts in particular could [...] become effective instruments in the hands of powerful industrial and commercial overlords enabling them to impose a new feudal order of their own making upon a vast host of vassals (p. 640).

Kessler recognized the prior importance of a principle like freedom of contract in a modern capitalist economy not just for its ethical value, but also rather for its practical consequences: a "contract is a private affair and not a social institution" (p. 630). This premise did not prevent him from asking whether it was possible to apply the principle literally even in the presence of an increasing use of contracts of adhesion, concluding that

> [T]his will not be the case so long as we fail to realize that freedom of contract must mean different things for different types of contracts. Its meaning must change with the social importance of the type of contract and with the degree of monopoly enjoyed by the author of the standardized contract (p. 642).

By contrast, competition between sellers should push them to offer the most efficient clauses in equilibrium. This view is well represented in Posner (1986):

> If one seller offers unattractive clauses, a competing seller, wanting sales for himself, will offer more attractive clauses. The process will continue until the clauses are optimal (p. 127).

E. D'Agostino, *Contracts of Adhesion Between Law and Economics*,
SpringerBriefs in Law, DOI 10.1007/978-3-319-13114-6_2

US federal courts have sometimes overridden signed contracts. In William v. Walker-Thomas Furniture Co. (1965) the court stated that when the less-powered party signs a "commercially unreasonable agreement" without any knowledge of its content, "it is hardly likely that his consent [...] was given to all the clauses".[1]

Such courts have stressed that the presence of a monopoly increases the risk of unfair clauses[2] and have usually referred to the notion of unequal bargaining power as relevant in order to not enforce contract clauses.[3] During the 1970s, some courts have considered unequal bargaining power as a case of "economic duress."[4] This interpretation allowed courts to intervene not only in the presence of a monopoly, but also whenever sellers offered the same clauses[5] since, under these conditions, those clauses offended public policy, as stated in Shell Oil Co. v. Marinell.[6] However, courts have rarely used market power to override contracts; they have usually concluded that standard clauses are enforceable whenever the existence of unequal bargaining power has not been proved.[7] It is the natural consequence of provisions that have given courts discretion whether to enforce "unreasonable" clauses and to justify overriding by defining unreasonable clauses.

2.2 The Critics to the "Market Structure" Hypothesis

The "market structure" hypothesis has been criticized on both empirical and theoretical grounds, which will be analyzed in sequence.

2.2.1 Theory

The critics to the "market structure" hypothesis on a theoretical point of view start from the general consideration that it is probably misleading to explain why sellers include standard clauses in their contracts by looking at the structure of the market, and more precisely at how much market power sellers can exploit.

---

1 Walker-Thomas, 350 F.2d, 449–450.

2 See Henningaen v, Bloomfield Motors Inc., 32 N.J. 358, 388–391 161 A.2d 69, 86–87, (1960); Clinic Masters Inc. v. District Court, 192 Colo. 120, 124, 556 P.2d 473, 475–476 (1976).

3 See C & J Fertilizer, Inc v. Allied Mut. Ins. Co., 237 N.W.2d 169 (1979).

4 See Austin Instrument Inc. v. Loral Corp., 29 N.Y.2d 124, 272 N.E.2d 533, 324 N.Y.S.2d 22 (1971). See also Dawson (1947).

5 See Equitable Lamble Corp. v. IPA Land Dev. Corp., 38 N.Y.2d 516, 523, 344 N. E.2d 391, 396, 381 N.Y.S.2d 459, 464 (1976).

6 63, NJ 402, 307 A2d 598, 601, 1973. See also Rozeboom v. Northwestern Bell Telephone Co., 358 NW2d 241, 242, 1984.

7 See Lamoille Grain Co. v. St. Johnsbury & L. C. R. R., 135 Vt. 5, 9, 369 A.2d 1389, 1391, 1976.

A more plausible explanation is that standard clauses reduce transaction costs between the two parties. These costs would become very high if the seller had to bargain clauses and conditions with each customer individually.

On this point, Rakoff (1983) pointed out that firms have to minimize their costs in order to be more competitive. For instance, vertical integration of firms allows them to reduce transaction costs (in clauses of uncertainty, delays, and inevitable disputes of dealing with outside operators). However, integration cannot avoid (sometimes expensive) transactions with final customers that can be reduced only by using contract standardization. The parallelism with Coase's approach is evident. Using Trebilcock's (1976) words,

> [T]he fact that [...] a supplier's products are offered on a take-it-or-leave-it basis is evidence not of market power but of a recognition that neither producer – nor consumer – interests in aggregate are served by incurring the costs involved in negotiating separately every transaction. The use of standard forms is a totally spurious proxy for the existence of market power (p. 364).

This preliminary argument, however, does not say anything about how one-sided the content of standard clauses is and whether it may rely on market structure. In this sense, it is still an open question whether it might be true that a monopolist uses his market power to impose inefficient one-sided clauses to the detriment of his customers, whereas sellers in less concentrated markets have to compete not just on price but also on contract clauses that, even if standard and non-negotiated, will turn out favorable to their customers.

Theoretically, monopolists have an interest to maximize their profits and to do so they should have an interest to offer transparent friendly clauses if consumers are willing to pay more for them.[8] Using Rakoff (1983) argument,

> [I]t is more paradoxical than persuasive to say that the firms most likely to insist on their detailed form documents are those able to have their way on the simplest clause of all, price (p. 1219).

Kessler explained the increasing use of standard form clauses as the trend of modern capitalism toward monopoly. By contrast, Rakoff replied that in order to understand standard form contracts as an economic phenomenon characterizing actual transactions, market structure does not matter, but our attention must focus on more complex institutional and social environments in which firms work. Precisely, in light of this sort of consideration, Rakoff rebated Kessler saying that

> [T]he legally supported practice of using contracts of adhesion must be viewed as an institution that itself generates and allocates power - not market power in the traditional sense, but power nonetheless (p. 1229).

On the same viewpoint, Baird (2006) criticized the court tendency of basing unenforceability of standard form contracts on a strong inequality of parties'

---

[8] Indeed, we will see in Chap. 4 that a monopolist has always an interest to offer fully transparent efficient clauses if disclosure is not too expensive.

bargaining positions, stating that standardization has nothing to do with bargaining power.

Bebchuk and Posner (2006) proposed a different approach to explain the presence of standard form contracts in competitive markets as sellers' defense against opportunistic consumers. They argued that there exists an asymmetry between a professional seller and a consumer, since only the former cares about its reputation and, therefore, has no interest of treating its consumers badly since it would lose them; while the latter has no reputation to lose simply because its behavior will not become known in the market. In such a case, including some one-sided clauses will allow the seller to differentiate its behavior given consumers' behavior. As such, it will be expected to treat fair consumers better than required by contract clauses and to use one-sided clauses only against opportunistic consumers.

Gilo and Porat (2006) pointed out that the usage of complex contracts based on the adhesion of one party to the content drafted by the other party has several explanations compatible with competitive markets.

First, competitive suppliers may use boilerplate clauses for segmentation of consumers whenever they want to screen out some of them. In such a way, firms may propose boilerplate clauses to unwanted consumers only in order to increase their transaction costs and to discourage them from purchasing.

A second, more interesting explanation for sellers offering complex contracts is to make them difficult to understand and therefore to compare with other contracts offered by other firms. Such strategies may be used in oligopolies in order to create and/or strengthen entry barriers to other firms.

Another mentioned explanation for the usage of contracts of adhesion given by Gilo and Porat (2006) is sellers' willingness to send a signal to consumers that the contract or some of its clauses are not negotiable. They highlighted that sellers may use consumer-friendly clauses based on the fact that they do not read them and, therefore, cannot ask for their implementation since they do not know their content. It might help sellers to immunize the contract against court or law intervention.

D'Agostino and Seidmann (2009) proposed a comparison between a monopoly and a competitive market, and showed that inefficient clauses characterize both markets with a similar incidence, but the effect of public intervention crucially depends on market structure in an opposite way than what economic theory suggests: a monopolist is the only player who actually gains from regulation, whereas consumers may be better off in competitive markets if the proportion of naïve consumers is small enough.

Friedman (2013) showed that competition is "a reason for more scrutiny of contract terms, rather than less", especially when there are enough naïve consumers. This aspect will be analyzed in detail in the next chapter.

2.2.2 *Empirical Evidence*

Empirically, it is a matter of fact that standard form contracts are ubiquitous, even in competitive markets. Raiser (1961) warned that an incorrect and unfair use of standard form contracts could take place not only in case of a monopoly, but also in competitive markets whenever the two parties have a different legal knowledge.

Priest (1981) examined the warranties offered for 62 products of different types of household appliances, such as refrigerators and washing machines, in relation to the industry concentration data and found that in those industries characterized by a few firms with high market share the usage of standard clauses is not more frequent than in other industries with more firms sharing the market. Furthermore, he did not find any relationship between the level of industry concentration and the degree of warranty coverage, even though his analysis did not search for an eventual effect of market concentration on prices.

More recently, Marotta-Wurgler (2008) confirmed the usage of boilerplate clauses even in competitive markets. Focusing on the market for software licenses, she showed that prices are sensitive to market structure, but the severity of clauses used in the agreements is not. She analyzed a sample of 647 hand-collected End User License Agreements (EULAs) of standard pre-packed software sold online by software publishers through their corporate website. This includes EULAs from established software publishers like Microsoft and Apple as well as hundreds of smaller, less-known firms.

Marotta-Wurgler gathered data on market share of individual companies in different software markets as well as the overall concentration of those markets from various sources. She estimated market shares and concentration measures using a recently developed methodology that uses Amazon.com "sales rankings" to estimate sales. Standard measures of competitive conditions include market share, at the company level, and concentration ratios and the Herfindahl-Hirschman index (HHI), at the market level.

Marotta-Wurgler defined a clause as biased toward the seller if it is more pro-seller than the default rules of the UCC, and more pro-consumer if it is more pro-consumer than those default rules. Starting from this basic setting, she found that firms in more concentrated markets and with more market power are more likely to charge higher prices, all else equal. However, she also found that the relative bias of the EULAs is about the same for most markets, independent of their level of concentration.

2.3 Doesn't Market Structure Matter at All?

This work embraces the skepticism about the market structure hypothesis, but for different reasons than those invoked by the main critics analyzed above.

Suppose a simple model like that presented in the Appendix of the previous chapter, with sellers informed about consumers' reservation prices for different levels of quality. In order to isolate the effect of market structure, we will assume that consumers are all sophisticated.[9]

Looking at a monopoly, absent any fine print and any reading cost, the only seller should be able to price discriminate by offering efficient clauses charging a price equal to consumers' reservation level in order to maximize his own utility. Conversely, competitive sellers should offer efficient clauses at the minimum price with consumers enjoying the entire market surplus.

Suppose efficient clauses are also those turning out consumer friendly, as assumed by the *Efficiency Condition* (see the previous Appendix). If some clauses are hidden in fine print and consumers have to pay a reading cost to become fully informed, it paradoxically reduces the monopolist's power because, even though he still knows consumers' reservation price, he is not able to price-discriminate. Precisely, assuming that the only seller has no alternative than offering contracts of adhesion with fine print, equilibrium-beliefs consistency deters a monopolist from charging the highest price for friendly and efficient clauses: for consistency requires that consumers believe that clauses are friendly, so they would always accept without reading. Then, a monopolist could profitably deviate to offering unfriendly clauses at the same price to get even higher payoffs trusting on the fact that consumers will not read. Then, every equilibrium turns out inefficient.

For similar reasons, in a competitive market consumers cannot enjoy friendly and efficient clauses at the minimum price: it makes the equilibrium equally inefficient.

What is said implies that consumers never read with certainty in equilibrium in any market. It affects parties' payoffs in an opposite way than what the traditional theory may suggest in the following sense. We will show in the Appendix that both markets are characterized by mixed-strategy equilibria in which sellers mix between friendly and unfriendly clauses, and consumers mix between reading and accepting without reading. It makes the equilibrium price fluctuate between the production cost and the consumers' reservation level for friendly clauses, with both sellers and consumers earning positive payoffs. Accordingly, on the one hand, a monopolist loses from using fine print because he cannot charge the profit-maximization price; on the other hand, competitive sellers gain because they would get 0 without.

This simple reasoning proves that no equilibrium can exist in which sellers always offer friendly clauses, but unfriendly clauses are ubiquitous, according to Marotta-Wurgler's (2008) evidence. More importantly, competitive sellers have a stronger incentive than a monopolist to include standard (and possibly unfriendly) clauses in fine print, as this is the only way to get positive payoffs in equilibrium.

However, we will show in Chap. 4 that market structure crucially and surprisingly affects the seller's incentive to disclose fine print: if disclosing is cheap enough a monopolist would have always an interest to disclose fine print and to

---

[9] We will relax this assumption in next chapter.

include friendly clauses, whereas competitive sellers always lose from disclosure and prefer to include fine print.

Market structure will also turn out crucial to interpret the effects of regulation. We will see in Chap. 5 that, although regulation aims to impose efficient clauses, it benefits sophisticated consumers only if sellers are competitive; whereas it cannot benefit and may harm them if the seller is a monopolist.

Appendix

We now use the game-theoretical model presented in the Appendix of the previous chapter, and solve the game searching for (symmetric) equilibria in both a monopoly and a competitive market.

As already highlighted in the chapter, we assume that consumers are all sophisticated: this assumption will be relaxed in the next chapter.

As a benchmark case, we first prove that the equilibrium would be efficient in both markets if consumers were able to read fine print at no cost (viz. $k = 0$).

Result 2.1 (Free reading)
If $k = 0$ then in equilibrium both a monopolist and competitive sellers offer friendly clauses and charge, respectively, u_h and c. Consumers accept and get 0 if they face a monopolist, whereas they get all the market surplus if they face a competitive seller. These equilibria are efficient.

Intuition
Not reading is weakly dominated because $k = 0$. Consumers' reservation prices for a friendly and an unfriendly contract are, respectively, u_h and u_l (where $u_h > u_l$) so that neither an unfriendly contract charging more than u_l nor a friendly contract charging more than u_h can be offered in equilibrium since consumers would reject.

A monopolist earns at most u_l from an unfriendly contract and $u_h - c$ from a friendly contract. The Efficiency Condition implies that $u_h - c > u_l$, so a monopolist has always an interest to offer a friendly contract. Consumers accept and earn 0.

Competitive sellers cannot offer an unfriendly contract at any price $p < u_l$ since another seller could attract all consumers by offering a friendly contract and charging a price p' such that $u_h - p' > u_l - p$ and this price always exists because $p < u_l < u_h$.

In turn, sellers must offer a friendly contract and competition will force them to charge the lowest possible price $p = c$. Consumers accept and earn $u_h - c$, whereas sellers earn 0.

Let now assume that the reading cost is strictly positive (viz. $k > 0$).

Result 2.2 (Monopoly)
a. A monopolist offers an unfriendly contract charging $p = u_l$ and consumers accept earning 0 in the only pure strategy equilibrium. Both parties get positive payoffs. This equilibrium is inefficient;

b. If the reading cost is small enough and u_h is large enough, a monopolist mixes between friendly and unfriendly clauses charging $p \in (c, u_h - k)$ *; consumers mix between reading and accepting without reading. Every player gets positive expected payoffs. This equilibrium is inefficient.*

Intuition

a. Belief consistency excludes an equilibrium in which a monopolist offers a friendly contract charging any $p \le u_h$: for consumers would always buy without reading and, since they would not read, the monopolist would profitably deviate to an unfriendly contract charging the same price in order to economize on the production cost c.

Conversely, there is an equilibrium in which the monopolist offers an unfriendly contract charging u_l. Since consumers accept [resp. reject] without reading at any price $p \le u_h$ [resp. $p > u_l$], no deviation to any other unfriendly contract is profitable for the monopolist. He cannot deviate to a friendly contract if consumers believe that it is rather unfriendly (see *adverse inference*, Sect. 1.7).

This equilibrium is inefficient because sellers offer unfriendly contracts (see the *Efficiency Condition*, Appendix of Chap. 1);

b. Consumers are indifferent between reading and accepting without reading only if they get the same payoff from both strategies. This is feasible only if the monopolist does not offer friendly or unfriendly clauses for sure, but mixes between the two alternatives. Call γ the consumers' belief that a contract is friendly. In order to mix, the monopolist must get the same payoff from both contracts: it implies that $p > c$, otherwise the monopolist will never offer a friendly contract; and $p < u_h - k$, otherwise consumers would not read as they would get less than *0* because $\gamma < 1$. Consumers get $\gamma u_h + (1 - \gamma)u_l - p$ if they accept without reading and $\gamma(u_h - p) - k$ if they read, so that they are indifferent only if

$$p = u_l + \frac{k}{1-\gamma} \tag{2.1}$$

They do not deviate to not buying without reading only if they get positive payoffs in equilibrium, that is, $\gamma u_h + (1 - \gamma)u_l - p > 0$. Substituting for p, this condition that is satisfied for some values of $\gamma \in (0, 1)$,[10] precisely:

$$\gamma \in \left(\frac{1-Y}{2}, \frac{1+Y}{2}\right), \tag{2.2}$$

where

$$Y = \sqrt{1 - \frac{4k}{u_h - u_l}} \qquad \text{requires } k \le \frac{u_h - u_l}{4}.$$

[10] γ must be greater than 0 and lower than 1 to allow both consumers and the monopolist to mix. Suppose otherwise: consumers would never read and would either not accept to pay more than u_l if $\gamma = 0$ or would accept at any $p \le u_h$ if $\gamma = 1$. As a result, the monopolist would never offer a friendly contract.

A monopolist earns $p - c$ if he offers friendly clauses and $(1 - r)p$ if he offers unfriendly clauses, where r is the probability that consumers read. Therefore, to be indifferent it must be

$$p - c = (1 - r)p$$
$$\Rightarrow r = \frac{c}{p}$$

where $p > c$ in order to assure that the monopolist gets a positive payoff. A monopolist does not deviate to an unfriendly contract charging exactly u_l if $p - c > u_l$, which requires $\gamma > 1 - k/c$. This last condition is satisfied at least for the highest value of γ in condition (2.2) if either $k > c$ or $k < c$ and

$$u_h > u_l + \frac{c^2}{c - k}$$

Adverse inference (see again Sect. 1.7) excludes any other deviation to a friendly contract charging any out-of-equilibrium price.

This equilibrium is socially inefficient because the monopolist offers unfriendly clauses only with some positive probability and consumers pay the reading cost with some positive probability (see again the *Efficiency Condition*, Appendix of Chap.1).

Result 2.3 (Competition)
a. Competitive sellers offer an unfriendly contract charging 0 *and consumers accept earning* u_l *in the only pure strategy equilibrium. This equilibrium is inefficient;*

b. If the reading cost is small enough and $u_l > c$, *sellers mix between friendly and unfriendly contracts charging* $p \in (c, u_h - k)$; *and consumers mix between reading and accepting without reading. Both sellers and consumers get positive payoffs. This equilibrium is inefficient.*

Intuition
a. Suppose that all sellers offer an unfriendly contract charging 0 and consumers accept. Sellers earn 0 and consumers earn u_l. Sellers cannot deviate to charging a price greater than 0 since other sellers would make all sales. No seller can profitably deviate to a friendly contract: for they should charge more than c in order to get positive payoffs, but consumers would not buy if they adversely infer that the deviating contract is unfriendly (see *adverse inference*, Sect. 1.7).

This equilibrium is inefficient because sellers offer unfriendly contracts (see the *Efficiency Condition*, Appendix of Chap. 1);

b. Again, as shown for the monopoly (see Result 2.2b above), sellers can mix between reading and accepting without reading only if consumers mix between reading and accepting without reading, and vice versa: precisely, sellers and consumers must get the same payoff from both their own strategies. Therefore, conditions

(2.1) and (2.2) as found in the previous Result at part b apply for the competitive market as well, where $p > c$ assures that sellers get positive payoffs, and always holds if $u_l > c$; whereas $p < u_h - k$ assures that consumers read with positive probability.

No seller has an interest to charge a price lower than the equilibrium range because consumers would infer that such contract includes unfriendly clauses, and would reject. Similarly, no seller has an interest to deviate to a friendly contract charging more than the equilibrium range of price because consumers do not expect such offer in equilibrium and would not trust the seller.

We now exclude a deviation to an unfriendly contract. To gain from such deviation, the deviating seller should be able to attract all consumers. It requires that the deviating contract must include a price q such that

$$\begin{aligned} &\gamma u_h + (1-\gamma)u_l - p < u_l - q \\ &\Leftrightarrow q < p - \gamma(u_h - u_l) \end{aligned}$$

where the left-hand side on the first row is consumers' expected utility in the mixed strategy equilibrium, and the right-hand side is consumers' utility from switching to the deviating seller. That seller would therefore get strictly less than q, which turns out unprofitable if

$$q < \frac{p-c}{N} \tag{2.3}$$

Since $p > c$, condition (2.3) is satisfied if $q < 0$, which requires

$$\gamma \in \left(\frac{u_h - Z}{2(u_h - u_l)}, \frac{u_h + Z}{2(u_h - u_l)}\right) \tag{2.4}$$

where

$$Z = \sqrt{\frac{(u_h - 2u_l)^2 - 4k(u_h - u_l)}{2(u_h - u_l)}} \, requires \, k < \frac{(u_h - 2u_l)^2}{4(u_h - u_l)}$$

It is easy to show that

$$\left(\frac{u_h - Z}{2(u_h - u_l)}, \frac{u_h + Z}{2(u_h - u_l)}\right) \subset \left(\frac{1-Y}{2}, \frac{1+Y}{2}\right),$$

so that condition (2.4) proves the claim. This equilibrium is socially inefficient because the monopolist offers unfriendly clauses with some positive probability and consumers pay the reading cost with some positive probability (see the *Efficiency Condition*, Appendix of Chap. 1).

Chapter 3
Lack of Sophistication

3.1 Naïvety and Psychology

Till now, we have assumed that consumers hold homogeneous preferences and are sophisticated, that is they behave rationally, taking into account the possibility that an eventual second clause may not contain any warranty. We now relax the last assumption and include naïve consumers into the analysis, where naïve consumers are those who hold a priori fixed beliefs about clauses in fine print, and therefore do not read.[1] In order to understand this last point, it will be helpful to distinguish, as psychologists do, between "salient" and "non salient" attributes (see Korobkin 2003).

The former are those attributes that consumers favor in their purchasing decisions, (such as price, number of items and so on); the latter are those attributes that consumers do not usually prioritize and, if included in some clauses, remain not read (such as warranties, liability exclusions, add-on prices, and so on). As logical consequence, sellers have an economic incentive to provide salient attributes at the efficient level of quality in terms of both form and content in order to make consumers willing to buy; while they have an incentive to make nonsalient attributes favorable to themselves only insofar as including them in fine print that consumers usually do not read.

On a different point of view, Ben-Shahar (2009) made a provocative reasoning that it is actually nonreaders who should be considered rational arguing that

> [S]pending effort to read and to process what's in the contract boilerplate would be one of the more striking examples of consumer irrationality and obsessive behavior (p. 18).

In this sense, the author suggested that the decision of not reading fine print rather implies the individual's desire not to get the best legal clauses, but just to buy "economy goods" and not "first class" clauses. It would also explain why such consumers care of price only.

---

[1] We have introduced the notion of naïvity in Sect. 1.3.2.

E. D'Agostino, *Contracts of Adhesion Between Law and Economics*,
SpringerBriefs in Law, DOI 10.1007/978-3-319-13114-6_3

Although ironic and maybe offbeat, Ben-Shahar's (2008) approach is not so far from being true in the sense that it is true that consumers could be happy to buy a good without reading every clause but if and only if price is not greater than their evaluation of an "economic good," to be intended as a "low quality good". Indeed, we allow for such a behavior in our models (see the Appendix of the previous chapter). By contrast, a consumer who pays a price higher than her evaluation for a low quality good without reading every clause cannot be considered rational even using Ben-Shahar's benevolent interpretation.[2] That is what we will hence refer to as a naïve (or not fully rational) consumer.

In first approximation, it can be said that increasing the number of clauses makes the contract more complex and requires a higher level of cognitive effort to understand its meaning. Psychologists have shown that consumers' behavior can be influenced by contract complexity in the sense that they try to minimize this effort. In particular, when consumers deal with complex decisions it seems that they react adopting a simple strategy: in our case, they do not read. Olshavsky (1979) demonstrated that when people are asked to choose between two alternatives each with four attributes, they analyze both very carefully. When attributes become 10 or 15, some of them are not taken into account. Malhotra (1982) interviewed people in order to collect information on their preferences about houses and apartments. He presented different alternatives of houses among which people were asked to choose. He found that accuracy in finding the house which better corresponds to needs (according to the profile given during the interview) is constant at a very high level when each alternative is presented with no more than 10 attributes and significantly decreases when the number of attributes goes up to 15 or 20. In general terms, as the number of alternatives and/or attributes increases, the percentage of information used to make the final choice decreases. Similarly, Grether et al. (1986) argued that when the decision set is relatively small, people do not experience problems and can make the choice corresponding to their own interests.

Given the strong evidence confirming such a theory, psychologists have also investigated why a person gives attention to some elements and not to others. Frances Luce et al. (1997) distinguished voluntary attention from involuntary attention. It can be said that people voluntarily give attention to those elements or facts they care for. For instance, they may guess that such elements are crucial in order to maximize their utility functions; at the same time, it may happen that some other elements not previously taken into account come by chance into consumers' consideration only at a later time.

Moreover, the authors also underlined that it might be the case that the lack of attention registered in individual decisions is only apparent and reflects an interior conflict that pushes people to take their attention away from certain attributes simply because taking a decision about them is too hard. Suppose that people

---

[2] However, we have shown in the Appendix of Chap. 2 that rational consumers may accept without reading with some positive probability in equilibrium for given levels of price higher than u_l. It is consistent with the notion of rationality because the game prescribes that in equilibrium consumers' payoff from accepting without reading is equal to their payoff from reading.

have to choose between alternative goods with different attributes, all of which considered very important (like safety and efficiency). In situations like this, the authors claimed that people face too much stress when involved in compensatory decisions, hence labeled as "emotion laden." Usually it is contract clauses that limit consumers' right to be compensated in case of damages caused by the product or forbid consumers to appeal to a public court (such as forum selection clauses). As a result, people usually react by ignoring such clauses in order to avoid stressful comparisons. Such removal effect is also favored by the fact that these clauses cover eventualities that are (or are perceived as) very unlikely to occur. Then, consumers who ignore nonsalient clauses may act as if they held optimistic or pessimistic beliefs about them.

3.2 Naïvety and Law

According to Korobkin (2003), efficiency requires not only that consumers are aware of the content of the contract they are signing but also that they take into account this information as relevant for their purchasing decisions. The same definition also refers to the concept of rationality: what we call naïvety can be also intended as lack of rationality in purchasing decisions.

If some clauses are considered salient and some others nonsalient in most consumers' point of view, only the latter category requires special attention by lawyers and courts since it is easy for the drafter to "manipulate" their content to the detriment of unaware consumers, whereas clauses in the former category can follow the general provisions of the law of contracts.

Even though limited to nonsalient clauses, the role of law and court intervention becomes very delicate in the presence of naïve consumers because the impact of a regulation on naïve preferences and actions is unpredictable.

Using Korobkin's (2003) words,

> The large body of evidence that human decision-making and choice deviates systematically from the usual law-and-economics assumptions of utility maximization, self-interest, and (often) wealth maximization, requires consequentialists to replace their default preference for unregulated markets with a greater initial agnosticism concerning the relative institutional competence of markets and government intervention (p. 1293).

Korobkin's solution is to use different approaches depending on whether clauses are salient or nonsalient. Salient clauses should be left to parties' autonomy, whereas nonsalient clauses should be verified by government institutions, and eventually amended or not enforced.

However, this solution is not always easy to implement because whether a clause is salient or nonsalient may depend on the other clauses as well. For example, saliency of clauses like warranties and customer assistance is certainly influenced by the price charged for the good on sale, that is by definition the most salient clause of every contract.

However, it does not mean that consumers cannot be naïve when they buy cheap products, e.g., opening a bank account is cheaper than signing a mortgage contract with a bank. Rather, the notion of naïvety we want to incorporate in the analysis is not that consumers voluntarily decide to skip reading those clauses they consider nonsalient. We rather consider the nonunlikely case that some consumers do not realize the presence of some clauses in the contract, so that they are not able to evaluate whether these clauses are salient or nonsalient. This approach is easier to model and able to capture naïvety as a general phenomenon.

If the consumer is not expert in legal subtitles and cannot realize the risk involved in signing without reading, we cannot say whether she thinks that those nonread clauses are salient or nonsalient, interesting or time-consuming, useful, or pointless. Under these circumstances, if she signs she will simply give a blanket assent giving up even the opportunity to read.

In this case, public intervention should not necessarily make consumers aware of every clause, including those they consider nonsalient, but it should at least educate naïve consumers about the physical presence of some clauses in the contract so that they can decide at least whether they are salient or nonsalient.

Naïve consumers may accidentally become unaware free riders and enjoy good contract clauses because there are enough sophisticated consumers in the market who push sellers to offer friendly and efficient clauses. This argument has become popular among lawyers who claim that regulation is effective if it at least increases the proportion of informed consumers to a critical mass, able to influence sellers' decisions. This view, well known in the literature as "informed minority" hypothesis, will be analyzed in details in Chap. 5.

3.3 Naïvety and Economics

Economics usually assumes that agents are rational. Possibly not symmetrically informed about the state of the world or other circumstances directly affecting their utility, but at least rational. In a world characterized by asymmetric information, the less informed party is rational if she is aware of her weak condition and forms beliefs about the more informed party's actions. It does not necessarily imply that the stronger party is able to exploit the weaker, but asymmetric information usually leads to inefficient outcomes and for this reason it is traditionally recognized as a market failure. For example, in the market for lemons proposed by Akerlof (1970) trade may not take place in equilibrium because, contrary to sellers, consumers cannot know the quality of second-hand cars on sale and may decide not to buy at any price if the expected quality of cars is not high enough to make trade profitable given the price. This equilibrium is inefficient as long as consumers' evaluation for a car of a given quality level is higher than seller's evaluation for the same car.

The example shows that rationality balances informational gaps and is able to protect the weaker party from the stronger party's possible exploitation, although it is not able to assure an efficient outcome.

However, if the less informed party is naïve, that is nonfully rational, then she cannot defend herself from the more informed party who can totally exploit his information power. Turning back to Akerlof's example, if consumers do not care about the quality of the second-hand car they will to buy or do not take into account the risk of buying a second-hand car, then trade could take place with sellers charging inefficient high prices which naïve consumers possibly accept.[3]

Armstrong and Chen (2009) presented a variant on Varian's (1980) model in which some consumers randomly choose a seller without taking care of market price and substitute consumers' inattention on price with consumers' lack of attention to quality. They modeled a competitive market with $N \geq 2$ firms offering a good that can turn out either high or low in quality. Producing a low quality good costs 0 to firms, whereas producing a high-quality good costs $c > 0$. All consumers observe price, but only a fraction $\lambda \in (0, 1)$ observes quality. Attentive consumers' evaluation is 0 for a low quality product and for a high-quality product. No reading cost is involved in the model, so that authors can conclude that only high (low) quality would be produced if $\lambda = 1$ ($\lambda = 0$), whereas the presence of heterogeneous consumers allows only for an asymmetric equilibrium in pure strategies in which some firms offer low quality charging 0 and others offer high-quality charging c. At the same time, the only symmetric equilibrium is in mixed strategies for firms mixing between high and low quality and charging $p \in (p_0, v)$. The authors referred to this last equilibrium and analyzed the effects of possible policies tending to either make more consumers attentive or the market more competitive. They showed that under the first policy firms are less likely to cheat, by offering low quality, and the social welfare increases, whereas under the second policy cheating firms are almost one half and the effect on welfare is ambiguous.

Our analysis is complicated by the presence of reading costs so that no consumer, even if sophisticated or attentive, can freely observe fine print. It may push sellers to offer low quality even if all consumers were rational (using Armstrong and Chen's terminology, if $\lambda = 1$), as shown in the previous chapter.

According to Armstrong and Chen (2009), it cannot be said that naïve consumers do not care of nonsalient attributes at all or less than sophisticated consumers; in other terms, there is no reason to assume that all consumers share the same evaluation about the corresponding contract clauses. Rather, naïve consumers simply do not realize the risk involved in fine print or trust the seller and believe that fine print always contains friendly clauses. There might be also consumers who hold pessimistic a priori beliefs, that is they do not trust the seller and believe that fine print always include unfriendly clauses. As a consequence, they always reject the contract without reading.

Ellison and Ellison (2009) generally discussed the problem of consumers' bounded rationality that firms can exploit. More precisely, the authors examined Internet transactions where price search engines and obfuscation interact together to make a price search more difficult and sometimes not convenient. Therefore, in

[3] For a deep analysis of consumers' naïve beliefs see Huck and Zhou (2011).

contrast with the traditional economics of information disclosure which predicts that disclosure takes place since high-quality firms have an interest to differentiate themselves from others by making consumers fully informed of their offers, the authors emphasized that firms in real environments are not prone to disclose their offers, especially those clauses regarding add-on goods. According to Lal and Matutes (1994), add-on prices can be considered as those prices regarding additional or complementary goods not observed by consumers when choosing to buy the base good. It allows firms to offer the base good at a very low price in order to attract consumers and, at the same time, to make high profits from high add-on prices.

Ellison and Ellison gave some examples of how these add-on prices work, especially in Internet transactions. Shipping costs are an example of how sellers are able to offer a product at several different prices. Consumers usually use price search engines in order to find retailers ordered by the category of goods sold and by price, such that for each category those retailers who offer the lowest price appear first. The authors suggested that sellers prefer lowering as much as possible their prices for low quality goods (which work as "loss-leaders") in order to attract consumers' attention to their shops, and try to redirect their purchases to medium- and high-quality goods. The analysis is both theoretical and empirical. The authors presented two different theories of how obfuscation can raise sellers' profits: the first being a standard search model in which obfuscation raises searching costs and therefore reduces consumers' awareness; the second being a price discrimination model in which obfuscation, instead of reducing consumers' awareness, prevents it from hurting sellers' interests. Model predictions have been tested and confirmed using data regarding eight product categories (four regarding computer memory modules and four regarding central processing units or CPUs) sold on the web by a price search engine (Pricewatch).

3.4 Market Structure and Naïve Consumers

We have already mentioned a few papers focusing on the combined effect of market structure and consumer naïvety.[4]

D'Agostino and Seidmann (2009) proposed a model where sellers can chose between simple and complex contracts or they may offer a menu of different contracts: simple contracts do not contain fine print and are governed by default rules, e.g., provided by contract law; complex contracts include hidden clauses that may turn out default (as those a simple contract refers to), but may turn out either onerous or favorable to consumers. The authors showed that sophisticated consumers never gain from the presence of enough naïve consumers if the market is a monopoly because the only seller has an interest to offer onerous contracts at high

[4] See Sect. 2.3.

price in order to exploit the latter category. On the other hand, sophisticated consumers are not affected by the presence of naïve consumers because in equilibrium they never pool, that is they trade with different sellers offering different contracts. It implies that the presence of enough sophisticated consumers cannot protect naïve.

Friedman (2013) obtained similar results in a model where sellers are allowed to offer each a single complex contract, and consumers may turn out either naïve or sophisticated. He found that if both sellers and naïve consumers are numerous enough, sellers are more likely to offer onerous clauses in order to exploit naïve consumers. It allows the author to conclude that "competition is reason for more scrutiny of contract terms rather than less."

In the Appendix, we will come back to the game theoretical model searching for equilibria in both a monopoly and a competitive market with some naïve consumers. All other assumptions are common to the previous chapters.

We will see that if enough consumers are naïve and believe that complex contracts contain friendly clauses then sellers will include inefficient unfriendly clauses irrespective of market structure. It implies that competition would not again allow for efficient clauses. It seems in further contrast to Kessler (1943). Such effect, already evident in the previous case with sophisticated consumers only, is trivially emphasized by the presence of naïve consumers: sellers have never an interest to offer friendly clauses in equilibrium if enough naïve consumers believe that every contract is friendly, so that they are happy to buy without reading.

It also implies that, contrary to Diamond (1971) and the previous chapter, price cannot exceed the Bertrand level in the competitive market (viz. $p = u_l$), so that sellers earn 0 in every equilibrium. It suggests that competitive sellers exploit naïvety, but only lose from the presence of enough naïve consumers as they get 0 in every equilibrium, whereas they could get positive payoffs in the class of mixed strategy equilibria if consumers were all sophisticated (see Result 2.3b). Also sophisticated consumers lose from the presence of some naïves in a competitive market as their payoffs cannot exceed the evaluation for a simple contract. Precisely, they get u_l in equilibrium from an unfriendly contract, whereas they would get higher payoffs in equilibrium in which sellers mix between friendly and unfriendly contracts and consumers mix between reading and accepting without reading (see again Result 2.3b).

Turning to a monopoly, the more naïve consumers are in the market the higher the equilibrium price: a result that is consistent with Marotta-Wurgler's (2008) evidence. Conversely, if naïve consumers are few enough, they are not able to influence the equilibrium outcome, which corresponds to what we found in the Appendix of the previous chapter.

To conclude, it seems that the presence of naïve consumers does not turn out decisive, unless they are the strong majority.

Appendix

We again use the model presented in the appendix of Chap. 1 assuming that a fraction $\theta > 0$ of consumers is naïve (or nonfully rational) and the others are sophisticated.

Precisely, we assume that naïve consumers hold optimistic beliefs about fine print, meaning that they a priori believe that every contract includes friendly clauses. As shown in the previous chapter, we refer to the notion of sophistication as synonymous of rationality.

We present (symmetric) equilibrium outcomes in a monopoly and a competitive market in sequence under the same assumptions made in the Appendix of Chap. 1.

Result 3.1 (Monopoly)
a. A monopolist offers an unfriendly contract and charges (1) $p = u_l$ if there are a few naïve consumers in the market (viz. θ is small enough), or (2) $p = u_h$ if naïve consumers are numerous enough (viz. θ is large enough). All consumers buy if charged u_l, whereas only naïve consumers buy if charged u_h. In both cases, the equilibrium is inefficient.

b. If θ is small enough, there exists a mixed strategy equilibrium as such characterizing the game with sophisticated consumers only in which naïve consumers always accept without reading.

Intuition
a. Suppose the monopolist offers an unfriendly contract. He has no interest to charge less than u_l when because all consumers would accept at that price. However, he knows that naïve consumers will accept to pay up to u_h without reading because they believe that fine print include friendly clauses; on the other hand, the monopolist knows that sophisticated consumers will reject the offer if charged more than u_l. Thus, a monopolist earns θu_h from an unfriendly contract when he charges u_h, and u_l from an unfriendly contract if he charges u_l. Trivially, he will go for the contract that assures the highest profit, so that he will charge u_h if $\theta > u_l/u_h$, and u_l otherwise.

Sophisticated consumers always get 0; naïve consumers believe to earn 0 in both cases but in fact they earn $u_l - u_h$ in the former case.

Conversely, there cannot exist an equilibrium in which the monopolist offers a friendly contract charging up to u_h. Consumers, including those who are sophisticated, would buy without reading, and the monopolist could profitably deviate to inserting unfriendly clauses at the same price to economize on the production cost c.

The equilibrium is inefficient because the monopolist offers unfriendly clauses (see the Efficiency Condition, Appendix of Chap. 1);

b. It comes from the previous chapter that sophisticated consumers mix between reading and accepting without reading only if the monopolist mixes between friendly and unfriendly clauses. We know that naïve consumers never read in equilibrium because they hold a priori optimistic beliefs about fine print. Therefore, it turns out that this equilibrium can exist at similar conditions found in the Appendix of Chap. 2 (see Result 2.2b) only if naïve consumers are few enough to not influence the monopolist's behavior. Conversely, if naïve consumers are numerous enough, then the monopolist has always a profitable deviation to an unfriendly contract charging u_h, even if it will attract naïve consumers only.

Result 3.2 (Competition)

a. Irrespective of how many naïve consumers are in the market, competitive sellers offer an unfriendly contract and charge 0;

b. If θ is small enough, there exists a mixed strategy equilibrium as such characterizing the game with sophisticated consumers only in which naïve consumers always accept without reading.

Intuition

a. Suppose that sellers offer an unfriendly contract and charge 0. They cannot deviate to charging a higher price because consumers would not buy. Suppose now that a seller deviates to offering a friendly contract: for this deviation to be profitable he has to charge slightly more than c and no consumer would buy. Precisely, sophisticated consumers do not buy if they believe that every out-of-equilibrium contract is unfriendly (see *adverse inference*, Sect. 1.7), and naïve consumers still match with a seller charging 0 because they believe that *every* contract is friendly.

On the other hand, no equilibrium exists in which (some) sellers offer friendly clauses: all consumers (including sophisticated ones) would accept without reading, and each seller could profitably deviate to an unfriendly contract charging the same price.

b. If naïve consumers are few enough they are not able to influence the equilibrium outcome that remains unchanged and follows the same line of that presented in the Appendix of the previous chapter (see Result 2.3b) with sophisticated consumers only.

Conversely, mixed strategy equilibria cannot survive if naïve consumers are numerous enough because each seller could profitably deviate to an unfriendly contract charging a slightly smaller price to attract naïve consumers.

Chapter 4
Voluntary Disclosure of Clauses

4.1 How to Disclose Contract Clauses

A third important element invoked for the application of the unconscionability doctrine is that contracts of adhesion usually include clauses written in a very technical and incomprehensible language for consumers.

In truth, this complaint does not say anything about the quality of clauses hidden in fine print, like warranties or other accessory services, which may turn out even favorable to consumers, although obscure. It raises an obvious question: why should a seller hide consumer-friendly clauses in obscure fine print?

The answer relies on the obvious consideration that standard clauses are necessary given the complexity of modern commerce that makes too costly and, in turn, impossible for parties to negotiate every clause. Think of warranties: in real transactions it is not usually the presence of a warranty that is hidden, but rather clauses and conditions at which the warranty works. Then, even though a warranty is formally offered, clauses and conditions that are too strict make it substantially impossible to be used, such that it is alike to no warranty being given.

If personalized contracts cannot be a feasible alternative to contracts of adhesion, Korobkin (2003) suggested that the alternative could only consist in "law-imposed default clauses invoked to fill the gaps in the contract the parties negotiate." (p. 1205). Korobkin warned that in order to justify an external intervention by law, contracts of adhesion have to be recovered under the spectrum of market failures.

We have already mentioned in Chap. 2 that no market, even though competitive, can be considered exempt from the risk of inefficient one-sided clauses. As long as consumers have not free access to every part of the contract (due to the reading costs), an asymmetric information process arises in favor of the drafter party who might include one-sided inefficient clauses in equilibrium. As a result, the market certainly fails.

Korobkin (2003) found the reason of this market failure in consumers' lack of sophistication, which we have discussed in the previous chapter. If enough

E. D'Agostino, *Contracts of Adhesion Between Law and Economics*,
SpringerBriefs in Law, DOI 10.1007/978-3-319-13114-6_4

consumers do not put attention to read contract clauses referring to some attributes they consider as non-salient, then sellers have no incentive to offer efficient clauses. It would also explain why competitive markets suffer of inefficient outcomes as well as more concentrated markets.

What is worthwhile to think of is whether sellers may find it profitable to voluntarily disclose their clauses in a non-regulated market. Above all, what sounds interesting is that voluntary disclosure may become a third way between boilerplate and public intervention to assure an efficient outcome or, al least, to reduce inefficiency.

Absent any law that makes inefficient clauses not enforceable, it is likely that sellers who voluntarily decide to disclose their contracts have to bear some cost.

We have already said in Chap. 1 that reading standard clauses is expensive for consumers, whereas writing them is relatively cheap for sellers. However, disclosing standard clauses requires an additional cost for sellers if they really want to make consumers fully informed. Indeed, to be effective, disclosure has to solve the problem related to consumers' unawareness as a consequence of asymmetric information, usually identified in the fact that they sometimes sign without reading some or all contract clauses.

If consumers are sophisticated, that is they care of what included in fine print and realize the risk involved in signing without reading, then to be effective disclosure should be able to cut off the reading costs and let consumers read clauses at no cost.

If consumers are naïve, that is they consider some clauses as non-salient or they do not realize the risk involved in signing without reading, then disclosure should refer to both the form and the content of standard clauses. Precisely, consumers should be first convinced that some clauses are more salient than what they would have thought, and/or warned about the physical presence of pre-printed clauses. Then, they should be made aware of the content of fine print without paying the cost to read them.

It looks like a labor of Hercules.

However, it is well known that consumers are very sensitive to some market practices. The simplest, though not necessarily cheapest way to attract naïve consumers' attention is investing in advertising. A seller who decides to "educate" their customers by advertising must provide the clauses that consumers like more, such as friendly warranty conditions, friendly forum selection clauses, and other accessory services that impose additional costs to the seller. Then, an advertising seller must bear the advertising cost plus the production cost for friendly and usually expensive clauses. It is therefore possible that the expected benefits from investing and competing in advertising, that is attracting as many consumers as possible, are smaller than the costs of making consumers aware, and therefore willing to use friendly clauses in their own interest to the detriment of the seller. We will analyze in next section the effect of clause disclosure on naïve consumers and the huge literature on this point.

Disclosure could be replaced by seller's reputation. Precisely, reputation should reduce the incentive for the seller to include unfriendly clauses in fine print in order to maintain a high level of trust among their customers, especially if sophisticated, without imposing additional costs to sellers but the cost of including friendly clauses.

However, the effect of reputation in the presence of contracts of adhesion risks to be less strong or even pointless if clauses in fine print are considered non-salient or consumers are unlikely to experience their content especially for those clauses referring to some situations which are very unlikely to happen. Even if we focus the attention to sophisticated consumers who care of the possibly unfriendly content of fine print, the main problem is again that they usually do not read boilerplate.

Under these circumstances it is easy to show that sellers cannot gain from reputation as much as they would if consumers were fully informed of clauses without reading or if reading were cheap enough.

Trivially, high-quality sellers are those who can and should invest more in reputation. Suppose a seller offers friendly clauses, like a warranty or insurance, but consumers do not read them. If clauses in fine print do not come in use (because the good works properly or the service is correctly delivered) then consumers cannot experience how friendly the contract is, and cannot take it into account for future transactions. As a result, the seller does not gain so much from offering friendly clauses. In Sect. 4.3 we will analyze the effects of voluntary disclosure when consumers are all sophisticated. We will also show that, contrary to the conventional wisdom, a monopolist is more willing to disclose and to offer efficient clauses than competitive sellers.

4.2 Voluntary Disclosure When Some Consumers Are Naïve

There is a large literature focusing on the effects of asymmetric information when the less informed party is not fully rational or sophisticated.

Schwartz and Wilde (1983) discussed the general problem of price searching and showed that in the presence of enough consumers who compare sellers' offers before buying from one of them, competition will lead to an efficient outcome by pushing sellers to offer good clauses at the lowest possible price. On a similar line, Shapiro (1995) argued that in the presence of "myopic" (to be intended as synonymous of naïve) consumers, competitive firms would have an interest to educate them by disclosing their contracts, offering efficient clauses. Also Armstrong (2008) agreed in the possible incentive for sellers to disclose all their prices as they could increase their profits more by increasing prices during the bargaining process rather than by a "rip-off".

In contrast, Gabaix and Laibson (2006) argued that, in the presence of a fraction $\alpha < 1$ of myopic consumers,[1] firms may have no interest to educate them about add-

[1] Gabaix and Laibson (2006) define "myopic" those consumers who are not fully sophisticated. This clause can be considered synonymous of "naïve" which will be used in our model. Precisely, Gabaix and Laibson's definition of myopic consumers corresponds to what we have referred to as "optimistic" consumers in the previous chapter.

on prices. The reason found by the two authors is that those firms are not able to attract consumers by advertising them, since educated consumers continue on buying from those sellers who shroud add-on prices having now enough knowledge to exploit the contract by substituting away from future use add-ons at a certain effort level. Gabaix and Laibson developed a game-theoretical model of three periods. In period 0 firms decide simultaneously a price for the base good, a different price for add-ons and whether to make add-ons shrouded or unshrouded. The first option may imply hiding add-ons in fine print, while the second option simply consists into advertising consumers about that price. In period 1, consumers enter a shop. Sophisticated consumers (fraction $1 - \alpha$) decide whether to buy taking into account add-ons, if unshrouded, or forming beliefs about them, otherwise. Myopic consumers do not look at add-ons if shrouded while just a fraction $\lambda \in (0,1)$ of them observes add-ons if unshrouded, and becomes sophisticated. The authors defined them "informed myopes"; conversely, those who do not understand shrouding and therefore remain uninformed (fraction $1 - \lambda$) are identified as "uninformed myopes". If the seller shrouds add-ons, no consumer can observe them and only the fraction $1 - \alpha$ of sophisticated consumers takes them into account; conversely, when the seller unshrouds add-ons, also a fraction λ of informed myopes will observe them. Therefore, unshrouding means enlarging the number of sophisticated consumers shared by all firms.

If add-ons are shrouded (unshrouded), sophisticated consumers (sophisticated consumers and informed myopes) set also the effort level to use in order to take add-ons away from future use if they will decide not to buy them.

In the case of shrouded add-ons, sophisticated consumers form their expectation about the price, and pay the substitution effort if it is lower than the price they expect to be charged for add-ons. When add-ons are unshrouded, both sophisticated and informed myopes will compare the substitution effort with the observed price for add-ons.

If a firm i shrouds (unshrouds) add-ons, after buying the base good, all consumers observe add-ons and decide whether to buy them; those who have decided to bear the substitution effort will not buy. Precisely, sophisticated consumers rationally believe that the seller will set the monopoly price for add-ons, so that they will decide to pay the substituting effort.

Gabaix and Laibson (2006) characterized symmetric equilibria of the game as follows:

a. For low values of α, sellers shroud add-ons and tend to set a very low price for the base good and a monopoly price for add-ons, which becomes the profit center and balances eventual losses coming from the low price offered for the base good. This equilibrium is also inefficient since sophisticated consumers have to pay the substitution effort;
b. For high values of α, sellers unshroud add-ons and charge a relatively cheap price for the basic good, according to the degree of competition, and a price for add-ons equal to the substitution effort. In such equilibrium all consumers buy add-ons.

The intuition is straightforward: suppose that some sellers unshroud add-ons, and some others do not. Sophisticated consumers would prefer buying from those with shrouded prices: in such a way, sophisticated consumers enjoy the low price for the base good and are able to avoid the high price for add-ons by paying the substituting effort. Therefore, in the presence of a high enough fraction of myopic consumers, no firm has an interest to disclose its contract.

Translating the analysis to the general case of contracts of adhesion, add-ons are not the only element possibly included (or shrouded) in fine print.

Furthermore, consumers have the chance to "unshroud" clauses by themselves because, although hidden in fine print, these clauses are included into the contract and therefore readable (even at some cost); by contrast, in Gabaix and Laibson (2006) the only possibility for consumers to know the price for add-ons is that the seller unshrouds it, and the only way to protect themselves from a very high unknown price for add-ons is to pay a substitution effort e. In this sense, such substitution effort plays a role similar to what we refer to as reading cost.

4.3 Voluntary Disclosure When Consumers Are All Sophisticated

Let now come back to a market in which consumers are all sophisticated, so that they decide to accept without reading after having looked at the price and taken into account the correspondent risk. In this case, disclosure is effective if it cuts off (or significantly reduces) the reading costs and allows consumers to be fully aware of every clause (almost) for free.

If the disclosing cost is relatively cheap it is straightforward to think that, regardless of how concentrated the market is, every seller should be willing to disclose and to offer efficient clauses.

On the one hand, a monopolist wants to maximize his profit and by disclosing efficient clauses he is able to get all market surplus minus the disclosing cost. In details, disclosing the contract allows a monopolist to raise the price up to consumers' reservation level for a friendly contract. If such price minus the production and the disclosing costs is higher than the reservation price that consumers are willing to pay for unfriendly clauses, then disclosure is efficient and a monopolist always gains from disclosing as his profits raise up. On the other hand, competition should push sellers to offer those clauses that consumers value more in equilibrium and to make them fully transparent in order to attract as many consumers as possible.

Some of these intuitive results are confirmed by the classic literature on voluntary disclosure of quality saying that

(1) If disclosing is costless, a seller will always disclose in equilibrium (Grossman and Hart 1980; Grossman 1981; Milgrom 1981); and

(2) If disclosing is costly, only high-quality firms will have an interest to disclose (Viscusi 1978; Grossman and Hart 1980).

This literature usually assumes the existence of only one firm of many hypothetical types, depending on the quality they sell. Few papers consider a competitive market, usually a duopoly, where more than one firm actually exists. Examples can be found in the works of Levine et al. (2009) and Board (2009). Levine et al. (2009) compared a duopoly and a cartel, and showed that disclosure of quality in equilibrium is socially excessive in both markets, but surprisingly less under a duopoly, where firms disclose only if quality exceeds a threshold level. They also found that welfare is higher under a cartel if the disclosure cost is relatively small, and under a duopoly in the opposite case.

Board (2009) focused on a duopoly with firms selling the same product of different qualities. He proved the existence of a partial disclosure equilibrium that differentiates his work from the main literature. Precisely he proved that if firms can disclose quality at no cost the high-quality firm always discloses in equilibrium, whereas the low-quality firm may not if disclosing would result in fiercer competition with the rival. Board argued that his results explain better the real world where some firms disclose and others do not, as suggested by Mathios (2000) for the salad dressing industry.

This literature usually starts from the assumptions (some of which look like rather unrealistic if applied to contracts of adhesion) that quality is exogenous, private information of sellers unless disclosed, and either not verifiable or verifiable only *ex post*. By contrast, in the special case of contracts of adhesion quality refers to the clauses of the contract and for this reason is rather endogenous as all firms can decide to insert high-quality clauses at some positive cost; moreover, consumers are allowed to verify the offer *ex ante* by reading the contract clauses at some positive cost. In the light of these different assumptions that dramatically change the impact of market structure on the disclosure strategy, our simple game theoretical model is able to show that:

(1) If the seller is a monopolist, the decision of whether or not to disclose does not depends on how expensive the disclosure costs are in absolute clauses, but relatively to the reading costs, so that a monopolist always discloses in equilibrium as long as doing so is cheaper than the cost for consumers to read; and
(2) Under competition, sellers do not disclose even if they offer friendly (viz. high quality) clauses, but prefer to include unshrouded fine print. Although counterintuitive, the reason beyond this result is quite straightforward. A disclosing seller must offer those clauses which consumers value more, but since consumers are fully aware of their content sellers cannot charge a price higher than the cost to produce friendly clauses plus the disclosing cost they bear to make them transparent. Thus, sellers cannot get positive profits from disclosing; conversely, they can charge a price higher than their costs if they include unshrouded fine print and mix between friendly and unfriendly

clauses, which consumers read with some positive probability.[2] If the price they should charge for a transparent contract in order to attract consumers is not high enough to compensate the increasing costs of disclosure, then such deviation turns out not profitable.

4.4 Is Disclosure at Least Effective?

We have emphasized that disclosure may take place under given circumstances if the related cost is cheap enough. How cheap it could be depends on the market structure, on consumers' sophistication, and other circumstances related to the nature of the transaction.

On the one hand, consumers would like that sellers disclose clauses, on the other hand sellers would like that consumers do not read non-transparent clauses. Certainly contract disclosure is not painless for sellers as well as reading is not painless for consumers. And even assuming that disclosure can be fully effective and makes clauses available to a free reading (viz. it makes reading costs equal to 0), using Coase's (1960) words, the crucial point becomes to avoid the most expensive cost.

As a result, efficiency requires that disclosure should take place only if its cost is lower than the cost that consumers bear to read fine print.

Disclosure is a way to exhume freedom of contract applied to contracts of adhesion. As long as the drafter party has disclosed clauses and conditions there is no more reason to appeal to the unconscionability principle and to invoke the unenforceability of the contract.

According to Katz (1990), an unrestricted duty to read should be applied whenever the seller speaks (so no limits or regulations should be imposed when speaking costs are sufficiently small); whereas an unlimited duty to read is Pareto inferior to a rule imposing a certain quality level when the seller remains silent, that is when speaking costs are sufficiently high. In Katz's terminology speaking corresponds to what we mean by disclosing.

Katz limited his analysis to monopolistic markets, but suggests possible extensions also to competitive markets.

We have also stressed that disclosure should force sellers to include efficient clauses in order to attract consumers (if the market is competitive enough) or in order to get the entire market surplus (if the market is concentrated enough).

However, if disclosure does not make reading significantly likely among consumers, then the seller's incentive to provide efficient clauses collapses and the risk of signing a transparent contract for consumers becomes even worse. Indeed, every "I agree" clicked or signature given to specific clauses becomes a seller's shield against consumers' complaint in front of a court of law.

---

[2] See the Appendix of previous chapters.

In the following Appendix we will focus on the extreme case that disclosure is fully effective, that is it makes every clause available to a free reading. It sounds odd, but it allows us to isolate the effect of disclosure in order to verify whether it would turn out efficient and consumer-protective. Accordingly, disclosure makes sophisticated consumers fully informed. The effect of disclosure on naïve consumers, however, is not so obvious. Different assumptions can be sustained on this point, such that naïve consumers may be never or always aware of disclosure. For the sake of completeness, we will assume that naïve consumers are not *ex ante* aware of disclosure, but some of them become aware *ex post* only if matched a disclosing seller. Being aware of disclosure means that a naïve consumer is able to understand the presence and the content of every clause at no cost, as well as sophisticated consumers. Being unaware of disclosure means that a naïve consumer still holds optimistic beliefs about the content of these clauses and precommits to buy without reading to the extent that she does not care of whether clauses have been made transparent or not.

The assumption sounds realistic because a naïve consumer is attracted by the lower priced contract, even if non-transparent. Conversely, if every contract includes the same price, some naïve may realize the presence of other clauses, provided that they are transparent.

We will see that results again turn out counterintuitive and confirm D'Agostino and Seidmann (2009) and Friedman (2013) conclusion that market structure matters in an opposite sense than what we expect. On the one hand, a monopolist has always an interest to disclose (provided that the related cost is cheaper than the reading cost) because he can raise the price up to consumers' reservation level. On the other hand, competitive sellers cannot gain from disclosure as they have to offer friendly and efficient clauses at the lowest possible price (equal to the production cost).

Sophisticated consumers may gain from disclosure only if they match a competitive seller, whereas they lose if they face a monopolist: the reason has to be found in the effect of disclosure on the equilibrium price. It sounds in further contrast to Kessler (1943). By contrast, naïve consumers cannot gain from disclosure even in competitive markets because they will never match a disclosing seller. These results hold if naïve consumers are few enough.

Market structure matters in an opposite way if enough consumers are naïve. On the one hand, a monopolist prefers to exploit them and does not disclose, so that consumers cannot gain; on the other hand, some competitive sellers disclose in order to attract sophisticated consumers, and other sellers do not disclose in order to attract naïve consumers. Since sellers have to offer friendly clauses if they disclose only sophisticated consumers are better off.

What emerges from these results is that, according to Ben-Shahar and Schneider (2014), disclosure is far to be the solution of consumers' problems when they handle a contract of adhesion.

Appendix

Suppose that sellers can decide to disclose their contracts at some cost $\delta > 0$.

To make disclosure attractive on a social point of view, we will assume that $\delta \leq k$: it means that disclosing the contract for a seller is cheaper than reading the contract for consumers.

We distinguish two cases. First, we assume that all consumers are sophisticated; then, we introduce a fraction $\theta > 0$ of naïve consumers.

Sophisticated Consumers

We start from some general results that always hold irrespective of the market structure.

Result 4.1

a. A disclosing seller must offer friendly terms.

b. No seller can offer a friendly contract with some positive probability in equilibrium without offering an unfriendly contract at the same price, unless he discloses.

Intuition

Proof is given by contradiction.

a. Suppose that a disclosing seller offers unfriendly terms. Consumers freely read unfriendly clauses and reject the contract if charged more than u_l. That seller then gets no more than $u_l - \delta$ and can profitably deviate to not disclosing at the same price to economize on the disclosing cost.

b. Part b. excludes (i) equilibria in pure strategies with a seller offering a non-transparent friendly contract; (ii) equilibria in mixed strategies where a seller does not disclose and mixes between friendly and unfriendly terms charging different prices, and (iii) equilibria in mixed strategies in which a seller offers friendly clauses and mixes between disclosing and not disclosing.

About (i), suppose that a seller does not disclose and offers a friendly contract charging $p > c$ without offering an unfriendly contract: consumers always accept without reading at any $p \leq u_h$ because they attach a probability equal to 1 that the equilibrium contract includes friendly terms, and the seller would profitably deviate to offering an unfriendly contract at the same price to economize on c.

A similar reasoning applies to (ii) if a seller does not disclose and mixes between a friendly contract charging p and an unfriendly contract charging $q \neq p$. For the seller being indifferent it must be $p = q + c$. Consumers could infer the contract quality looking at the price and would always accept without reading if $p \leq u_h$ and $q \leq u_l$ However, the seller could profitably deviate to an unfriendly contract charging p to economize on the production cost.

About (iii), the previous reasoning in (ii) also excludes an equilibrium in which a seller discloses with some positive probability. Suppose now that a seller offers a friendly contract and mixes between disclosing charging p and not disclosing charging q. To be indifferent it must be $p = q + \delta$. Consumers would accept any offer without reading for every price $p \leq u_h$, and the seller would profitably deviate to a non-transparent unfriendly contract charging q to economize on the production cost c.

In sum, a non-disclosing seller must mix between a friendly and an unfriendly contract charging the same price p. It is impossible if consumers always read or accept without reading because the seller would never offer respectively un unfriendly or a friendly contract. Then, consumers must mix between reading and accepting without reading.

Result 4.2 (Monopoly)
A monopolist always discloses and offers friendly clauses charging $p = u_h$. *Consumers accept and earn 0. This equilibrium is unique and efficient. A monopolist always gains from disclosure, whereas consumers can only lose.*

Intuition
A disclosing monopolist must offer friendly clauses (see Result 4.1): he has no interest to charge less than u_h because consumers would buy at that price and the monopolist would simply reduce his profits. The monopolist gets $u_h - c - \delta$. Suppose he deviates to a non-transparent contract. He cannot charge more than u_l if consumers infer that the deviating contract contains unfriendly terms. Such a deviation turns out unprofitable according to the *Efficiency Condition* because $\delta \leq k$.[3] It also proves that this equilibrium is efficient because friendly clauses are offered in equilibrium.

We now prove that this equilibrium is unique.

Result 4.1b excludes any other equilibrium in pure strategies or in mixed strategies unless the monopolist charges $p > c$ and mixes between friendly and unfriendly clauses, and consumers mix between reading and accepting without reading. The monopolist must charge less than $u_h - k$ in such a putative equilibrium, otherwise no consumer would read with positive probability in equilibrium. He would then get strictly less than $u_h - c - k$, and could profitably deviate to disclosing because $\delta \leq k$. A similar reasoning excludes an equilibrium in which the monopolist discloses with some positive probability.

Note that a monopolist gets $u_h - c - \delta$, and always gains from disclosure because $\delta \leq k$; whereas consumers get 0 and can only lose from disclosure as they would have got positive payoffs in some equilibria (see Result 2.2b for a comparison).

---

[3] The *Efficiency Condition* states that $u_h - c - k \geq u_l$ (see the Appendix of Chap. 1). It follows that $u_h - c - \delta > u_l$ because $\delta \leq k$.

Result 4.3 (Competition)

a. Sellers offer a transparent contract charging $p = c + \delta$, *and consumers accept. This equilibrium is efficient. No other equilibrium exists if the reading cost is large enough; otherwise,*

b. If the reading cost is small enough, sellers do not disclose and mix in equilibrium between friendly and unfriendly, both priced at some $p \in (c, u_h - k)$*; consumers mix between reading and accepting without reading. This equilibrium is inefficient.*

Sellers are unaffected by disclosure, whereas consumers gain from matching a disclosing seller.

Intuition

a. Proof follows the same line of that given for Result 4.2a. The only difference is in the equilibrium price that is lower than in a monopoly, and equal to sellers' costs. No seller can charge a higher price in equilibrium because the contract is transparent, so that consumer can compare the offers and always buy from sellers charging the lowest price. This equilibrium is efficient because sellers offer friendly clauses (see the Efficiency Condition).

b. Result 4.1b again implies that the only case to analyze is that with sellers mix between not disclosing and mixing between friendly and unfriendly clauses, and consumers mixing between reading and accepting without reading. Proof follows a similar line of that given for Result 2.3b, so that conditions (2.1) and (2.2) still apply with $u_l > c$ and $p \in (c, u_h - k)$ (see the Appendix of Chap. 2). We have just to exclude that deviating to either an unfriendly contract or to disclosing is profitable for sellers. In order to attract consumers, a disclosing seller should offer friendly clauses (see Result 4.1) charging a relatively cheap price q such that consumers prefer buying from him. It requires

$$\gamma u_h + (1 - \gamma)u_l - p < u_h - q$$
$$\Leftrightarrow q < (1 - \gamma)(u_h - u_l) + p$$

where the left-hand side of the first inequality is consumers' utility from a non-transparent contract and the right-hand side is consumers' utility from switching to a disclosing seller who charges q. The deviating seller would therefore get strictly less than $q - c - \delta$. The efficiency Condition implies that $(1 - \gamma)(u_h - u_l) + p - c - \delta > p - \gamma(u_h - u_l)$ because $\delta \le k$ where the right-hand side is a seller's payoff from deviating to an obscure unfriendly contract (see result 2.3b). Therefore, a sufficient condition to exclude every possible deviation becomes

$$q - c - \delta < 0$$

which requires

$$\gamma \in \left(\frac{2u_h - u_l - c - \delta - A}{2(u_h - u_l)}, \frac{2u_h - u_l - c - \delta + A}{2(u_h - u_l)} \right),$$

where

$$A = \sqrt{(c + \delta - u_l)^2 - 4k(u_h - u_l)} \text{ is well defined, if } k \leq \frac{(c + \delta - u_l)^2}{4(u_h - u_l)}$$

If $u_l < c + \delta$, it is easy to show that

$$\left(\frac{2u_h - u_l - c - \delta - A}{2(u_h - u_l)}, \frac{2u_h - u_l - c - \delta + A}{2(u_h - u_l)} \right) \subset \left(\frac{1 - Y}{2}, \frac{1 + Y}{2} \right),$$

proving the claim.

Note that sellers cannot gain from disclosure because they cannot charge more than their costs. At the same time, they do not lose because they still do not disclose and get positive payoffs in the equilibrium above in which they mix. By contrast, consumers gain from matching a disclosing seller as they get u_h- c - δ, whereas they would have got strictly less without disclosure (see Result 2.3 for a comparison).

Naïve Consumers

Let now assume that a proportion $\theta > 0$ of consumers is naïve, as well as we did in the previous chapter. We assume that naïve consumers become sophisticated, and therefore fully informed, only if they match a disclosing seller, except a proportion $\omega \leq \theta$ that always remains unaware. Accordingly, naïve consumers remain naïve (viz. $\omega = \theta$) if they match a non-disclosing seller. The last point implies that if competitive sellers charge different prices because only some of them disclose, then naïve consumers always buy from those charging the lowest price regardless of whether these sellers have disclosed or not.

Result 4.4 (Monopoly)
A monopolist always charges u_h. He discloses and offers friendly clauses if and only if θ is small enough. If θ is large enough, then a monopolist does not disclose and offers unfriendly clauses. A monopolist always gains from disclosure, whereas consumers can only lose.

Intuition
A monopolist could charge u_h for a fully transparent contract and would earn $u_h - c - \delta$ if he offers friendly clauses or $\omega(u_h - \delta)$ if he offers unfriendly clauses. If he deviates to a non-transparent contract, then he has to charge no more than u_l to

sell to all consumers, whereas he would sell to naïve consumers only if he charges a higher price. In either case, the monopolist would include unfriendly clauses getting either u_l or $\theta u_h > \omega(u_h - \delta)$. None of these deviation is profitable if θ is small enough and $u_h - c - \delta > u_l$. The last condition always holds in equilibrium because $\delta \leq k$ (see the *Efficiency Condition* in the Appendix of Chap. 1). Note that the monopolist never mixes between friendly and unfriendly contracts at the same price without disclosing for the same reasons presented in Result 4.2.

A monopolist gets $u_h - c - \delta$, and always gains from disclosure because $\delta \leq k$.

Consumers earn 0 if the monopolist discloses, so they cannot gain and sometimes lose in respect to those mixed-strategy equilibria in which they would have got a positive payoff (see Result 3.1 for a comparison).

Result 4.5 (Competition)

a. Sophisticated consumers trade with competitive sellers who disclose and offer a friendly contract charging c + δ, and naïve consumers trade with sellers who do not disclose and offer an unfriendly contract charging 0.

b. If θ is small enough, there exists a mixed strategy equilibrium as such characterizing the game with sophisticated consumers only, in which naïve consumers always accept without reading.

Sophisticated consumers alone gain from matching a disclosing seller.

Intuition

a. The specified strategies form an equilibrium if sophisticated consumers believe that a deviating seller who does not disclose offers unfriendly clauses (see *adverse inference*, Sect. 1.7). Sophisticated consumers trade with disclosing sellers charging $c + \delta$ and do not deviate to those charging 0 because $u_h - c - \delta > u_l$. Again, it comes straightforward from the *Efficiency Condition* because $\delta \leq k$. Naïve consumers are attracted by sellers who charge the lowest price and get u_l.

All sellers earn 0 and none of them can profitably deviate to charging higher price for either a transparent or non-transparent contract because they would not trade. By contrast, no equilibrium can exist in which all sellers disclose and charge $c + \delta$ because they could get a positive payoff by deviating to a non-disclosed unfriendly contract charging a slightly lower price to attract naïve consumers.

b. If naïve consumers are few enough they are not able to influence the equilibrium outcome that remains unchanged and follows the same line of that presented in Result 4.3b. with sophisticated consumers only.

Conversely, mixed strategy equilibria cannot survive if naïve consumers are numerous enough because each seller could profitably deviate to an unfriendly obscure contract charging a slightly smaller price to attract naïve consumers.

Note that sellers cannot gain from disclosure as they have to charge a price equal to their costs. At the same time, they do not lose because they do not disclose and get positive payoffs in some equilibria if both k and θ are small enough. Sophisticated consumers get $u_h - c - \delta$ and always gain from matching a disclosing seller as they would have got strictly less without disclosure. Naïve consumers never match a disclosing seller, so that they do not gain and do not lose from disclosure (see Result 3.2 for a comparison).

Chapter 5
Public Intervention

5.1 Introduction

We now analyze how legal systems have addressed the problems related to the usage of contracts of adhesion. In particular, we will compare a common law system, such as the US system, with a civil law system, such as the German system. We will also analyze how the latter has influenced the EU legislation culminating in Directive 93/13/EEC.

Generally speaking, there is a large consensus that every legal system must protect consumers against evidently unfair, non-negotiated clauses: the key question in examining different legal systems is how protective these measures should be.

Comparing the European and the US systems, we will note strong differences in the protection offered to consumers, as European laws are more protective than those in the US, so the former works as a regulation of clause content, whereas the latter mainly consists of a regulation of clause disclosure.

Nevertheless, we will note that courts in both systems (even in civil law countries, like Germany) have played an important role in identifying high-risk cases and have also used the market structure criterion, which we deny in this work, in order to regulate those markets where sellers exploit some market power.

5.2 The US System

According to Maxeiner (2003), US legislation has been based on two main principles: (1) contracts of adhesion are not a priority for the Government to intervene and (2) there is no way to balance the "freedom of contract" principle with "fairness of clauses." Such a conviction has left space only for weak protection against unfair clauses, especially in the past decades.

E. D'Agostino, *Contracts of Adhesion Between Law and Economics*,
SpringerBriefs in Law, DOI 10.1007/978-3-319-13114-6_5

5.2.1 From Unconscionability…

Section 2-302 of the Uniform Commercial Code (from now on, UCC) allows, but does not require the courts to override a clause they find "unconscionable." This means that the final decision becomes judge sensitive, bearing the risk of different treatments for different cases. This rule, initially formulated to be applied to contracts of adhesion only, was extended to any possible transaction by the 1960s, when the UCC became law across the country,[1] although in practice most of judicial cases in which it was invoked regarded standard clauses.[2]

On a first time, courts were inclined to apply a quite strict duty to read, so that a consumer who knows the existence (not necessarily the content) of some clauses and nevertheless decides to sign without reading cannot then claim that those clauses are unconscionable.

Different solutions have been taken into account only in extreme cases. *Henningsen v. Bloomfield Motors, Inc.*[3] regarding the disclaimer of warranty in the purchase of an automobile, is a representative case in which the unconscionability theory has been applied. The New Jersey Court of Appeals stated that:

> The gross inequality of bargaining position occupied by the consumer in the automobile industry is thus apparent. There is no competition among the car makers in the area of express warranty. Where can the consumer go to negotiate for better protection? Such control and limitation of his remedies are inimical to the public welfare and, at the very least, call for great care by the courts to avoid injustice through the application of strict common-law principles of freedom of contract.

Few years later, the Virginia Court rejected this doctrine in *Marshall v. Murray Oldsmobile Company, Inc.*[4] where the court stated that

> …A reading of the Henningsen case and a tracing of its questionable acceptance in other jurisdictions since it was decided in 1960 failed to convince us of the efficacy of following the action of the New Jersey Court. We are loath to make such abrupt changes in the settled law and reluctant to declare invalid the formal undertakings of parties for such vague reasons of public policy.

In the 1980s, some commentators argued that contemporary legislation had become obsolete because it had no provision about software and computer information.[5] Moreover, they argued that legislation provided so little protection for consumers that some attempts to modify it appeared necessary. Already in 1981 in

---

[1] The UCC is not law itself, but only provides recommendations of what laws should provide. It becomes law only if a state decides to give it enforcement. The first State that gave it enforcement was Pennsylvania in 1954. At the end of 1960s, almost all States gave it enforcement.

[2] Particularly, Slawson (1971) reported no case out of thousands involving a nonstandard clause. See also White and Summers (2005).

[3] 32 N.J. 358, 161 A2nd 69, 75, 1960.

[4] 204 VA 972, 154 S.E. 2nd 140, 1967.

[5] See Gomulkiewicz (1998).

Graham v. Scissor-Tail Inc,[6] the California Supreme Court stated that a standard contract is fully enforceable "unless certain other factors are present which […] operate to render it otherwise."

Courts have recently started applying the principle of freedom of contract less strictly. In *Philyaw v. Platinum Enterprises Inc.*,[7] the court refused to enforce an arbitration provision because consumers could not have bargained for better clauses even in the case in which they had understood arbitration clauses.

Courts have also started to override contracts without requiring both procedural and substantive unconscionability (see Chap. 1). In *East Ford Inc. v. Taylor,*[8] the court stated that in the presence of procedural unconscionability, it is not necessary to provide proof of the substantive component; conversely, in *Sosa v. Paulos*[9] and *Gillman v. Chase Manhattan Bank,*[10] courts came to the conclusion that gross disparity in clauses or substantively "outrageous" clauses are enough to support unconscionability, even without the procedural aspect.

However, the main courts' tendency is to ban clauses that cause "consumers' surprise," that has been included in the procedural unconscionability test. In *Kinney v. United Heathcare Services Inc.*,[11] the court found surprise in the fact that the employee could not have read the clauses in the employee handbook, and in *Villa Milano Homeowners Association v. Il Davorge,*[12] the clause under judgment was on page 67 of a 70-page contract.

In section 211(3), the (second) Restatement of contracts states that "where the other party—the drafter—has reason to believe that the party manifesting such assent—the nondrafter—would not do so if he knew that the writing contained a particular clause, the clause is not part of the agreement." Even though this rule focuses on drafter's expectation, in those few cases (mainly regarding insurance contracts) in which it has been applied courts have looked at the nondrafter party expectation.

Hillman and Rachlinsky (2002) suggested that such courts' interpretation makes the Restatement work a "reasonable expectation" test. According to the test, if the clause was outside the reasonable expectations of the person who did not write the contract, and if the parties were contracting on an unequal basis, then it would not be enforceable. Those who support the use of the test say that it can be assessed objectively looking at the prominence and the purpose of the clause, and at the circumstances surrounding contract acceptance. With respect to the unconscionability test where the notion of unreasonableness remains vague, this approach emphasizes consumers' expectation. However, according to Korobkin (2003), it

[6] 623 P.2d 165 (Cal. 1981).

[7] 54 Va.Cir. 364, 2001.

[8] 826 S2d 709, 715, 2002.

[9] 924, P2d 357, 361, 1996.

[10] NA, 73 NY2d 1, 534 NE2d 824, 829, 1988.

[11] 70 Cal App 4th 1322, 83 Cal Rptr 2d 348, 353, 1999.

[12] 84, Cal App 4th 819, 102 Cal Rptr 2d 1, 7, 2001.

does not help solve the question of whether a clause could be considered reasonable if consumers had not notice of it. Moreover, since the test bans any unusual and therefore not reasonably expected clause, it cannot be applied to those shrouded clauses that have become usual, and therefore expected, in certain type of transactions. For instance, in *Sparks v. St. Paul Insurance Co.*,[13] the court declared the contract enforceable since clauses were consistent with commercial reasonable standards.

Apart from these theoretical issues, the test is less easy to apply than the unconscionability test (see Chap. 1). Certainly, it does not help clarify what has to be always considered reasonable and what unreasonable, but requires (as well as unconscionability) a case-by-case analysis. What is certain is that the courts recognize the existence of an implicit agreement, "blanket" assent making enforceable any not unreasonable clause (Llewellyin 1960).

5.2.2 ... to the Theory of Mandated Disclosure

Despite the court tendency of saving freedom of contract as a general principle, following a different approach, closer to the European system (see Sect. 5.5), Leff (1970) and Slawson (1971) had already suggested a public solution to the problem of contract standardization. In particular, Leff pointed out that making standard form contracts unenforceable could have turned out dangerous, given the frequent usage of them in market transactions. Rather, he suggested a new government intervention requiring the maximum possible disclosure of clauses in order to ban those considered one sided. Thinking that such policy was not enough, Leff went further and proposed the introduction of a mandatory establishment of minimum contractual rights as an alternative to a judicial law based on precedence.

Similarly, Slawson (1971) proposed to build an "administrative law of contract." Based on the assumption that contracts are legitimated by the consent of parties, as well as any lawmaking act, he stated that since standard form contracts are not negotiated they should be submitted to judicial review as well as any lawmaking process not validated by a democratic process. Thus, Slawson proposed that judges should review standard form contracts according to a "nonauthoritative standard," defined as

> [R]easons, principles, or considerations possessing no legal authority within the jurisdiction but of greater generality than the law being reviewed and serving to demonstrate that it is in the public interest (p. 533).

In fact, there was a huge proliferation of pieces of law, acts, and principles imposing some standards of clause disclosure and applying to specific markets

[13] 100, NJ 325, 495 A2d 406, 414, 1985.

where the usage of fine print seems too detrimental for consumers. Examples in the US tradition are easy to be found.

In financial markets, the Security Act of 1933, the Securities Exchange Act of 1934 and the Investment Company Act of 1940 impose sellers to provide precise information about the product offered.

The Truth in Lending Laws of 1968 is, according to its own long title, "an Act to safeguard the consumer in connection with the utilization of credit by requiring full disclosure of the clauses and conditions of finance charges in credit transactions or in offers to extend credit…"

About warranties, the Magnuson-Moss Warranty Act of 1975 provides that a seller who wants to offer a warranty for a consumer product must fully and clearly disclose clauses and conditions applying to the warranty in an easily readable language.

The Nutritional Labeling and Education Act of 1994 requires that calories, cholesterol, total fat, and other important information must be in bold print to attract consumers' attention.

More recently, in 2009 the American Law Institute (ALI) approved the Principles of the Law of Software Contracts. ALI Principles apply to electronic contracts and, given the high risk of oppressive clauses, they encourage disclosure of clauses even before a shopper initiates a transaction (see section 2.02(c)).

Again in 2009, the US Congress approved the Credit Card Accountability, Responsibility and Disclosure Act with the scope of establishing "… fair and transparent practices relating to the extension of credit under an open end consumer credit plan, and for other purposes" (H.R. 627 (111th)).

These and other documents applying to specific contracts have built on a regulation focusing on mandatory disclosure in the US tradition with no or little attention to the content of standard clauses.

A policy that imposes sellers to disclose contract clauses is based on the assumption that consumers would like to read every page of the contract, but they do not because it turns out too hard or costly. However, according to Ben-Shahar (2008)

> … [T]he problem now is not only that the clauses are written in an incomprehensible language; the problem is that individuals do not know how to evaluate the content of the clauses – the contingent events for which many of the clauses apply (p. 21).

Is clause disclosure a strong enough incentive for sellers to provide efficient clauses? And, one step behind, does disclosure increase the likelihood that a consumer reads contract clauses? These two questions are closely and trivially connected because sellers would not insert expensive clauses, even though efficient, if consumers are not likely enough to read.

5.3 The "Informed Minority" Hypothesis

Nevertheless, it is hardly surprising that disclosure has been the favored regulatory choice to combat problems associated with imperfect information. After all, it is considered relatively cheap, nonintrusive, and thus does not risk ill-informed direct regulation of clauses and mandating standards. Moreover, it preserves consumer choice and it encourages sellers to compete on the basis of the information disclosed. For a disclosure regime to be effective, however, it must increase readership of contracts by a significant amount, and in addition, consumers and investors must be conscious and willing to change their decisions conditional on what they read.

The theory of disclosure-based regulation is fairly intuitive. By reducing search and reading costs, disclosure facilitates comparison shopping and increases the number of informed consumers. In principle, a disclosure regime can be beneficial even if it does not affect the behavior of most consumers; it can be effective even if most consumers do not read or compare shops based on what they read. What is required is that these regimes increase the number of informed consumers to a critical mass, sometimes called as "informed minority" (see Schwartz and Wilde 1981). If this critical mass of comparison shoppers exists, disclosure is claimed to be effective in sufficiently competitive markets, because sellers will have an incentive to satisfy the informed consumers. The uninformed nonreaders get a free ride to acceptable standard clauses. The argument requires that sellers are unable to discriminate between informed and uninformed consumers.

However, this view was rejected empirically and theoretically, as we will see now in details.

5.3.1 Critics to the "Informed Minority" Hypothesis: Theory

In this section, we will analyze some theoretical results that reject the main conclusions of the "informed minority" hypothesis.

Ben-Shahar (2009) pointed out that, even if this minority of readers exists, sellers will nevertheless use their bargaining power to charge higher prices if they cannot insert unfriendly clauses. However, the most likely scenario is a separating equilibrium in which different contracts are offered with different clauses and prices in order to attract different consumer groups. This solution may turn out even worse for the majority of nonreaders who will "pay the bill" for good contracts offered to and accepted by the few readers.

Che and Choi (2009) analyzed the effect of different interpretation rules (more precisely, the "duty to read" against the "duty to speak" regime) on equilibrium outcomes and social welfare when consumers show heterogeneous preferences on quality.

The authors showed that under a duty to read in which firms simultaneously decide price, quality and whether to speak, there exists a pure strategy equilibrium in which firms do not speak and offer low quality, and consumers accept without reading; or a mixed strategy equilibrium for some firms charging a high price and offering high quality with some positive probability and other firms charging a low price and offering low quality. Consumers who do not care about quality buy from a randomly matched low price firms, whereas consumers who care about quality match a high price firm and read with some positive probability.

Turning to the duty to speak regime, the authors consider possible policies, among which the so-called "mandatory speak" (MS) regime, when firms are forced to speak as preliminary condition to trade. By speaking sellers make it easier or less costly for consumers to read the contract.

However, since all firms must speak consumers are not able to infer quality without reading, so that they must incur the reduced reading cost. As a consequence, the equilibrium corresponds to that characterizing the duty to read regime with some firms mixing between high quality and low quality and charging a higher price, and others offering low quality and charging a low price. Again, consumers who care about quality trade with sellers charging the high price and mix between reading and accepting without reading; whereas consumers who do not care about quality accept a low-priced contract without reading.

The effect on social welfare of such policy compared to the duty to read regime is ambiguous: on one hand consumers pay a lower reading cost, and on the other hand sellers have now to bear the speaking cost. However, the authors underline that the "mandatory speak" regime is not fully efficient because all sellers must speak regardless of the quality they offer. Since speaking is not informative, even though the probability that consumers read is higher given the reduced reading cost, sellers do not find it profitable to offer high quality with certainty, but still mix between high and low quality.

5.3.2 *Critics to the "Informed Minority" Hypothesis: Empirical Evidence*

Empirical evidence on the effectiveness of disclosure regimes is piecemeal. A typical example can be the market for retail food. On the one hand, the introduction of mandatory calorie postings at chain restaurants in New York City decreased calorie consumption at Starbucks by a modest 6 % (see Bollinger et al. 2010). On the other hand, a study of the effect of the Nutrition Labeling and Education Act on the salad dressing market found a statistically significant decrease in sales in dressings with the highest fat content after the passing of the act. Naturally, if consumers do not read or understand the labels, such regimes will be less effective.

Turning to contracts of adhesion as a general category, Bakos et al. (2014) and Marotta-Wurgler (2012) analyzed the online market for software licenses and presented the results of a large sample of 47,399 households. Marotta-Wurgler (2012) used clickstream data on the visits of these households to a set of online software retailers over a period of 1 month in order to prove that the degree of disclosure has almost no impact on the rate at which consumers read EULA (End-user licence agreement, establishing the purchaser's right to use the software). The number of mouse clicks required for opening the related window on the screen measures the accessibility of EULA.

Results showed that no consumer accesses EULA when the company website requires six click wraps. The situation does not change much as disclosure increases. Of the 49,079 shopping visits to companies whose clauses and conditions require three clicks to be read, only 13 saw the EULA, corresponding to a rate of about three EULA accesses per 10,000 shopping visits (i.e., potential EULA accesses). When disclosure was improved and terms required just two clicks to appear on the screen, the readership rate actually fell down slightly, to around 1 in 9,000. When only one click was required, the readership rate increased but was still tiny: only about 1 in every 300 shoppers.

As a result, Marotta-Wurgler concluded that it is statistically true that increasing disclosure does increase readership, meaning that the rates of access to clauses and conditions do tend to increase when it requires "less effort," measured by the number of clicks required to find these clauses. However, increasing disclosure does not increase contract readership to any meaningful rate.

Bakos et al. (2014) found that EULA were accessed in only 55 of the 120,545 visits to software retailers (0.05 % of all such visits) and in 40 visits to freeware companies (0.14 %). The average number of words of clauses and conditions for retail products in the sample (unreported) is 2,277 with a standard deviation of 1,148 words. This is an interesting information given that the authors found that the average time spent on the page is 47.7 s and the median time is 29 s, meaning that the time spent in reading EULA relative to their length clearly shows that most readers do not read clauses in their entirety.

These arguments led the authors to the same conclusion, namely that data seemed inconsistent with the "informed minority" equilibrium.

5.4 Who Gains from Mandatory Disclosure?

Mandated disclosure has been so popular, especially in the US tradition that Ben-Shahar and Schneider (2014) complain that

> … [G]enuine analyses of mandated disclosure's costs and benefits are rare, a fact that seems to leave lawmakers unperturbed (p. 2).

They provocatively define this process of unconditional surrender to mandated disclosure regulation as "disclosurite."

On the one hand, it is certainly hard to sustain that disclosure produces the miraculous effect to make the contract so transparent to be available and easy to read for consumers.

On the other hand, it is not true that the cost of disclosure regulations is almost nonexistent. First, sellers have to comply with rules and procedure that may involve time and resources. Second, they face the risk to invest in additional high-quality services (like warranties, assistance, etc.) or expensive advertising with no certainty of attracting consumers' attention.

In sum, according to Ben-Shahar and Schneider (2014):

> Mandated disclosures typically address unfamiliar and complex issues. To provide the information a reasonable person would want to make a good decision, disclosers pile so much information on readers that they cannot possibly cope with the burden of understanding and analyzing what they have read. These problems are intensified by the fact that people are often no literate enough, or schooled enough in the complexities of quite specialized decisions, to use the information profitably. And to explain unfamiliar and complex choice, disclosures must often be written at a college reading level (p. 6).

Even assuming that clause disclosure is fully effective, that is it makes consumers able to read contract clauses at no cost, who gains from disclosure?

Again, the answer has to be contextualized in the market we have in mind because sellers may decide not to offer efficient clauses in equilibrium even assuming that friendly clauses are efficient (in our model it is assured by $u_h - c - k > u_l$).

However, offering friendly clauses does not necessarily mean that consumers are better off.

Precisely, if disclosure is not accompanied by a regulation on price, then paradoxically it may harm rather than protect consumers.

Suppose there is one seller only in the market and consumers are all sophisticated. In the previous chapter, we have shown that if the disclosing cost were cheap enough, a monopolist would voluntarily disclose if consumers could observe clauses for free. In this way, the monopolist would be able to get the entire market surplus by raising the price up to the consumers' reservation level. Mandatory disclosure would not change the final outcome, which is efficient but advantages only the monopolist with consumers getting 0. The same result holds if there are few enough naïve consumers. Suppose now that naïve consumers are numerous enough. Result 4.4 shows that a monopolist would not voluntarily disclose and would offer unfriendly clauses in order to exploit naïve consumers. If disclosure is mandatory, the monopolist must disclose, but still offer unfriendly clauses if enough naïve consumers remain such: they correspond to the proportion we have labeled ω (see the previous chapter and its Appendix). It implies that sophisticated consumers still lose from disclosure, whereas naïve consumers who become aware (proportion $\theta - \omega$) gain from disclosure since they would have accepted an unfriendly contract at the maximum price otherwise.

Turning to a competitive market, we have shown that sellers do not gain from disclosure because they must offer friendly clauses and lower the price down to their production costs. Then, the entire market surplus goes to consumers with sellers getting 0. Mandatory disclosure, however, will turn out protective for sophisticated consumers who enjoy low prices for a friendly contract, but not for naïve consumers. Precisely, not every seller offers friendly clauses because another seller could still exploit proportion ω of unaware naïve consumers by offering unfriendly clauses at a lower price. It implies that every equilibrium is asymmetric with some sellers offering high-priced friendly clauses and attracting sophisticated consumers, and other sellers offering low-priced unfriendly clauses, able to attract naïve consumers. All sellers charge no more than the production cost for the quality offered, so they earn 0 in equilibrium and cannot exploit naïvety. However, naïve consumers lose from disclosure because they either do not buy (if aware) or buy unfriendly clauses (if unaware).

5.5 The EU System

5.5.1 From the German Statute…

Before analyzing EU legislation, in particular about the 93/13/EEC Directive, it is important to retrace the main stages of German legislation and jurisprudence as the German system has influenced most of the Directive.

The German system was the first, among other European countries, to understand the problem of standard form contracts and to provide some measures to control their unfair use. As early in 1871, a Statute imposed mandatory liability in railroad agreements. However, the German Supreme Court excluded extensive application of the statute to other possible contracts in 1883, stating that, absent any legislation, the principle of freedom of contract prevented judges from intervening in favor of consumers by not enforcing standard form contracts. After the promulgation of the Civil Code in 1900, judges found the applicable law in section 138, stating that "A transaction that offends good morals is void," and in section 242 stating that "Obligations shall be performed in the manner required by good faith, with regard to commercial usage."[14] The courts' interpretation of these two rules, especially that about good morals, changed over time. In the 1930s and 1940s, the courts usually tended to adopt them in monopoly situations in light of the obvious consideration that consumers have no alternative to the monopolist's offer and have to accept it.

After the Second World War and the reintroduction of a democratic system, the courts started to identify good morals with the more general concept of good faith, abandoning monopoly situations as main cause of violations of section 138.

In section 305(1), the Statute defines standard clauses as "all contractual clauses preestablished for a multitude of contracts which one party to the contract (the drafter) presents to the other party upon the conclusion of the contract." The form and the position in which these clauses are included into a contract do not matter. The Statute consists of two principal parts, the incorporation control and the content

[14] See Dawson (1976), who compared German and US legislations.

control that correspond, respectively, to the notions of procedural and substantive unconscionability.

About the incorporation control, section 305(2) requires the drafter to give the other party notice of the clause and the opportunity to review it. In addition, for standard form contracts to be enforceable the nondrafter must give an explicit assent to their use. Section 305a provides some particular cases in which standard form contracts apply even in the absence of previous requirement. An important regulation about surprising clauses is included in section 305c(1) stating that they never form part of the contract. Section 305c(2) fixes a general rule about interpretation of unclear clauses: in that they must be interpreted against the drafter. Surprising clauses are those clauses such that "in the circumstances, in particular in view of the outward appearance of the contract, are so unusual that the contractual partner of the user could not be expected to have reckoned with them," section 305c(1). The absolute exclusion of force of these clauses is not motivated by their presumptive unfairness; rather, an unfairness test is not required at all. In this sense, unusual clauses are treated as presumptively unfair, without requiring an explicit test.

Another important provision is included in section 306(1): when some clauses are declared unenforceable, the remainder of the contract is still valid. Lawyers stress the importance of this rule that turns out in favor of consumers. By contrast, if the unenforceability of a clause (regarding clauses different from those that are necessary for the contract to exist) made the whole contract unenforceable, it would turn out dangerous for consumers who might need the good or service purchased and might therefore decide to accept the unenforceable clause.

In regard to the content control, section 307(1) states that standard form contracts are invalid if their content is contrary to the requirement of good faith, that is, when they provide an unreasonable disadvantage to the nondrafter.[15] But what is definitely new is the inclusion of two lists in sections 308 and 309 regarding, respectively, those clauses "whose validity depends on an evaluation" and those "whose invalidity is not subject to any evaluation." On one hand, the list included in section 308 that requires a validity evaluation is a guideline for courts; on the other, the list of banned clauses included in section 309 prevents the application of the law from becoming judge sensitive, at least in those cases recognized as the most dangerous.

Section 310(1) states that some rules, like those in sections 305(2) and (3), 308 and 309 do not apply to standard form contracts included in contracts among business people, that are subject to normal rules included in the Civil Code.

[15] Particularly, section 307(2)(1) presumes an unreasonable disadvantage whenever the standard clause deviates from a fundamental principle of any other applicable law; section 307(2)(2) presumes that an unreasonable disadvantage limits a benefit that the contract should provide.

5.5.2 … to the 93/13/EEC Directive

The Statute turned out very useful, and was applied in an enormous number of settlements. It remained a separate statute until January 1, 2002, when it became part of the German Civil Code. The Statute was later modified in order to harmonize it with the 93/13/EEC Directive (from now on Directive), but it was used as the main reference for the content of the Directive. In particular, the main difference between the German Statute and the Directive is that the former is a "contract model," in the sense that it applies to any contract. Conversely, the latter is a "consumer model," in the sense that it applies to those categories of contracts in which the nondrafter is a consumer, intended as a person involved in a nonbusiness transaction.

In further contrast, the first Draft of the Directive also applied to individually negotiated clauses. This provision provoked a strong reaction from German scholars who argued that such a rule would have destroyed the principle of freedom of contract. In the final version of the Directive, this provision was changed, and its application was limited to standard, non-negotiated clauses.

Another difference is that the Directive does not contain any specific provision about incorporation of standard form contracts into a contract, except a general rule included in Article 5 stating "clauses must always be drafted in plain, intelligible language." By contrast, the content control is the core of the Directive. In particular, Article 3 states that a clause can be considered unfair "if, contrary to the requirement of good faith, it causes a significant imbalance in the parties' rights and obligations arising under the contract, to the detriment of the consumer." Then, according to the German Statute, a list of 17 specific types of clauses that can be always considered unfair is included in an Annex, but the unfairness evaluation for any other clause not included in that list is left to national judges on a case-by-case basis. Article 6 states that unfair clauses shall not be enforced, while Article 7(2) states that once a clause is declared unfair consumer groups are authorized to bring actions "to prevent the continued use of such clauses."

It has to be taken in mind that the Directive is not law itself but must be applied by Member States, who are free to provide stricter protecting measures in favor of consumers. In this sense, the Directive provides only a minimum standard of protection that must be implemented by internal laws in every Member State. The EU Court of Justice has the duty to decide about several cases of presumptive nonfulfillment of the Directive against several States. In 2000, the Commission reported the level of its implementation in every Member State; after this report, the Court of Justice decided many cases ordering States to implement the Directive content. Despite the few differences, the Directive looked so similar to the German Statute that the German Parliament did not need to change the internal rule. After all, the general application to any contract of the internal law is perfectly consistent, albeit more protective, with the EU Directive.

The Commission also set up an accessible database (called CLAB), renewed every 5 years, including all legal decisions regarding unfair clauses. In the first 5 years only, the CLAB contained 7,685 cases[16] confirming that the Directive has been effective, in that it has given the courts a guideline that is easy to follow and allows them to intervene in a similar manner beyond different doctrinal interpretations.

In 1993, the Commission sustained published studies that have confirmed the use of standard form contracts in the Member States in several different markets, such as sales, the car rental market, banking service markets (like current accounts and consumer credit contracts) and insurance markets (civil liability for motor vehicles, home insurance) and markets for tourist services (rented accommodation, holiday clubs, package holidays, etc.). Since 1996, the Commission has also subsidized actions proposed by several consumer associations, that in many cases have successfully eliminated the use of some unfair clauses in some sectors, like the new technology market, car rental, and tourism markets.

The Commission has also subsidized a project (contract B5-1000/98/000021-DECO (P)) proposed by a Portuguese consumer association, in order to draw up, through negotiation with professional bodies, standard form contracts in five economic sectors (the sale and brokerage of real estate, time-share contracts, travel contracts, contracts for the purchase and sale of used cars, and contracts for the repair of vehicles) with a high rate of individual disputes over possibly unfair clauses. Negotiation has been successful in each sector, with the exception of time-share contracts.

Finally, the Commission has also favored an informational campaign in order to make people full-informed of the risk involved in some contracts and on their rights in case of unfair clauses.[17]

5.6 Who Gains from Mandatory Friendly Clauses?

Suppose that what we have referred to as an unfriendly contract contains vexatious, and therefore banned clauses, so that law imposes courts to substitute them with the correspondent consumer-friendly content.

Assuming that turning to a court is free for consumers, they have not to care anymore about the contract clauses, so that accepting without reading dominates reading as long as the price does not exceed consumers' evaluation for a friendly contract. A policy like this has the positive effect of making friendly clauses in a certain sense mandatory. We wonder whether it is enough to protect consumers.

---

16 Consumer Policy: Commission Aims To Update Unfair Clauses Data Base, Eur. Rep., section 2583, April 7, 2001.

17 The first information campaign was in 1995, regarding unfair contractual clauses and conditions about package holidays and overbooking in air transport. It was run in 11 Member States (B, D, E, F, G, I, IRL, LUX, NL, P and UK) and consisted of short messages broadcast by the national radio stations.

We will see in the Appendix that mandatory friendly clauses would raise welfare, while reducing sophisticated consumers' payoffs if the seller is a monopolist. It would mean that social welfare increases because the monopolist's utility increases. Therefore, if such a policy has the aim of protecting consumers it should be used only in competitive markets: a result that is mitigated if enough consumers are naïve. Such apparently perverse result relies on the fact that laws only interpret the second clause allowing the monopolist to adjust his price. Absent from any regulation on the salient attributes, above all the price, every regulation focusing on the non-salient attributes becomes useless in terms of consumer protection, if implemented in a monopoly.

Turning to a competitive market, mandatory friendly clauses turn out consumer protective because, absent from any asymmetric information process about contract clauses, consumers are sure to sign friendly contracts and competition makes the rest of the job, forcing sellers to charge low prices.

Although the effects of a regulation imposing friendly clauses (or banning vexatious clauses) look like similar to the effects of a mandatory disclosure regime, the latter policy turns out less efficient as it imposes a disclosing cost on sellers that makes price increase in the competitive market.

Appendix

We now analyze the effects of different public interventions, like those analyzed in the chapter. We start from a mandatory disclosure regime, roughly corresponding to the US system, and then we turn to a regulation about clause content, roughly corresponding to the EU system.

As well as we did in the previous chapter, we assume that disclosure makes the reading cost $k = 0$, so that sophisticated consumers become fully informed. Naïve consumers become sophisticated, and therefore fully informed, only if they match with a disclosing seller, except a proportion $\omega \leq \theta$ that always remains unaware.

About regulation on contract content, we assume that it makes friendly terms mandatory.

In both cases, in order to isolate the effect of regulation, we will assume that consumers do not experience any cost to go to a court to protect their rights.

First, we assume that all consumers are sophisticated; then, we introduce a fraction $\theta > 0$ of naïve consumers.

Mandatory Disclosure

We again limit the analysis to the case $\delta \leq k$, meaning that disclosing is cheaper than reading.

Result 5.1 (Sophisticated consumers)
A monopolist and competitive sellers disclose and offer friendly terms charging respectively u_h *and* $c + \delta$. *Consumers accept and earn respectively* 0 *and* $u_h - c - \delta$.

A monopolist gains from mandatory disclosure, whereas competitive sellers may only lose. Consumers never gain and only lose from a mandatory disclosure regime if they face a monopolist, whereas they never lose and always gain if they face a competitive seller.

Every equilibrium is efficient.

Intuition
Since disclosure is mandatory, no deviation to a nontransparent contract is feasible. Moreover, Result 4.1 excludes that unfriendly clauses are offered in a transparent contract. A deviation to a different price would turn out unprofitable in both markets: no seller can charge a higher price because consumers would reject.

Similarly to what said in the previous chapter for voluntary disclosure (see Result 4.2), a monopolist gets $u_h - c - \delta$ and always gains from mandatory disclosure. By contrast, competitive sellers get *0* and can only be worse off than in a free market with or without disclosure (see Results 2.3b and 4.3b). Consumers get 0 if they face a monopolist, so that they cannot gain and may lose in respect to those mixed strategy equilibria in a free market without disclosure where they would have got positive payoffs (see Result 2.2b). Conversely, they get $u_h - c - \delta$ if they face a competitive seller and get the entire market surplus. It means that they can only gain in respect to a free market with or without disclosure where sellers offer unfriendly contracts with some positive probability (see Results 2.3 and 4.3b). Efficiency comes from the fact that sellers in both markets disclose and offer friendly clauses (see the Efficiency Condition in the Appendix of Chap. 1).

Result 5.2 (Naïve consumers)
a. A monopolist charges u_h *and offers friendly clauses if and only if* ω *is small enough; otherwise, he offers unfriendly clauses at the same price. Sophisticated and aware naïve consumers accept only if offered friendly clauses: the former category never gains and sometimes loses from disclosure; whereas the latter category gains only if* θ (ω) *is large (small) enough, and may lose otherwise. Unaware naïve consumers accept every offer: they sometimes gain and sometimes lose.*

b. Proportion θ *of competitive sellers offers unfriendly clauses charging* δ*: they attract all naïve consumers and trade only with proportion* ω. *Proportion* $1 - \theta$ *of competitive sellers offer friendly clauses charging* $c + \delta$ *and trade with sophisticated consumers. Sophisticated consumers always gain from disclosure, whereas naïve consumers never gain and sometimes lose.*

Intuition
Deviating to a nontransparent contract is unfeasible because disclosure is mandatory.

a. A monopolist could charge u_h for a transparent contract and would earn $u_h - c - \delta$ if he offers friendly clauses or $\omega(u_h - \delta)$ if he offers unfriendly clauses as only proportion ω of naïve consumers will buy. Then, he offers friendly clauses if and only if $\omega < 1 - c/(u_h - \delta)$. Consumers get 0 in equilibrium, except proportion ω of naïve consumers who lose $u_l - u_h$. Comparing these results with those found in Result 3.1b without disclosure, it turns out that if θ is small enough, consumers cannot gain and sometimes lose from mandatory disclosure because they would have got positive payoffs in a free market in the class of mixed strategy equilibria. Conversely, if θ is large enough, no consumer loses and proportion $\theta - \omega$ now gains from disclosure as they reject and get 0, whereas they would have lost $u_l - u_h$ in a free market.

Comparing these results with those found in Result 4.4, we see that mandatory disclosure sorts out the same effects of a voluntary disclosure regime if θ is small enough: it comes straightforward from the monopolist's advantage to disclose in the latter case. On the other hand, if θ were large enough, the monopolist would not voluntarily disclose and would offer unfriendly clauses priced at u_h, which naïve consumers only would accept. It implies that a mandatory regime never harms and may help naïve consumers if ω is small enough, whereas it does not affect sophisticated consumers who always earn 0.

b. Competitive sellers get 0 in equilibrium and none of them can profitably deviate because every contract must be transparent and consumers would not buy from a deviating seller charging higher prices. Conversely, no equilibrium could exist in which all sellers disclose and offer the same clauses, either friendly or unfriendly. If they offer friendly clauses they must charge $c + \delta$ getting 0, and a seller could profitably deviate to an unfriendly contract charging a lower price (just above δ) to attract naïve consumers with proportion ω buying. If they offer an unfriendly contract they must charge δ getting 0, and a seller could profitably deviate to offering friendly clauses charging a price lower than $u_h - u_l + \delta$ to attract sophisticated consumers.

Naïve consumers get $u_l - \delta$, and can only lose if sellers must disclose because they would have got u_l for the same unfriendly contract in a free market with or without disclosure, and even more if θ is small enough in a mixed strategy equilibrium (see Results 3.2 and 4.5). On the other hand, sophisticated consumers get $u_h - c - \delta$, and since $\delta \leq k$ they always gain in respect of a free market without disclosure (see again Result 3.2); they never lose and sometimes gain even in respect to a free market with voluntary disclosure if θ is small enough (see again Result 4.5).

Mandatory Friendly Clauses

We now assume that sellers are free to disclose or to include fine print, but they must include friendly clauses. Every unfriendly clause will be override by court and substituted by a friendly clause.

Result 5.3 (Sophisticated consumers)
If friendly clauses are mandatory, then in every equilibrium no seller discloses, and:

a. A monopolist offers friendly clauses and is better off;

b. Competitive sellers offer friendly clauses and may lose.

c. Consumers accept without reading. They cannot gain but sometimes lose in a monopoly; while they always gain in a competitive market.

Intuition

No seller discloses in order to economize on the related cost.

a. A monopolist charges u_h for a friendly contract and consumers accept earning 0. The monopolist earn $u_h - c$ and is better off than in a free market with or without disclosure. In the former case, he would have wasted the disclosing cost (see Result 4.2); in the latter case, he would have got either u_l from an unfriendly contract (Result 2.2a) or less than $u_h - c - k$ in the class of mixed strategy equilibria (see Result 2.2b).

b. Competitive sellers must charge c for a friendly contract, else another seller could profitably undercut. Sellers get 0 in equilibrium and lose in respect of a free market with or without disclosure where they would have got positive payoffs in the class of mixed strategy equilibria (see Results 2.3b and 4.3b).

c. Consumers earn a non-negative (and sometimes positive) payoff when the seller is a monopoly in a free market without disclosure (see again Result 2.2b). Conversely, they earn 0 if friendly clauses are mandatory, so that they can only lose as well as in a free market with disclosure (see again Result 4.2).

Turning to a competitive market, consumers earn $u_h - c$ and gain from mandatory friendly clauses since they would have got lower payoffs in a free market with or without disclosure: indeed, Results 2.3b and 4.3b prove that sellers always charge more than c if they offer friendly clauses with some positive probability in equilibrium.

Result 5.4 (Naïve consumers)

If friendly clauses are mandatory, then in every equilibrium no seller discloses, and:

a. A monopolist always charges u_h. He gains only if $\theta < 1 - c/u_h$, and loses otherwise. Sophisticated consumers never gain and sometimes lose, whereas naïve consumers sometimes gain and sometimes lose.

b. Competitive sellers charge c and can only lose; consumers of both types always gain.

Intuition

Again, no seller discloses in order to economize on the related cost.

a. No other deviation is feasible for a monopolist since unfriendly clauses are not available. He therefore gets $u_h - c$. Comparing the monopolist's payoff with and without regulation, it turns out from Results 3.1 and 4.4 that if $\theta < u_l/u_h$ he gains from mandatory friendly clauses. Conversely, if $\theta > u_l/u_h$ he would have offered unfriendly clauses in a free market charging u_h, trading with naïve consumers only and getting θu_h. He therefore gains from regulation only if $\theta < 1 - c/u_h$, and loses otherwise.

All consumers get 0. If θ is small enough, consumers never gain and may lose in respect of mixed strategy equilibria where they would have got positive payoffs in a free market without disclosure. If θ is large enough, sophisticated consumers are unaffected, whereas naïve consumers gain as they would have lost $u_l - u_h$ in a free market with or without disclosure (see again Results 3.1 and 4.4).

b. No deviation is feasible or profitable for sellers, who get 0 in equilibrium. Consumers get $u_h - c$. Comparing this outcome with those characterizing equilibria in a free market with or without disclosure (see Results 3.2 and 4.5), sellers never gain and sometimes lose from mandatory friendly clauses; whereas consumers always gain since friendly clauses are offered at the lowest possible price: a condition that never arises in equilibrium in a free market.

Chapter 6
Concluding Remarks

We have provided a simple model examining some controversial issues related to the usage of contracts of adhesion, where the offer comes from sellers to consumers on a take-it-or-leave-it basis and consumers can verify the contract *ex ante* by reading clauses at some positive cost. We have analyzed the unconscionability doctrine, as traditionally applied to contracts of adhesion, and have criticized its main criteria: market structure, lack of sophistication, and contract complexity. We summarize our results as follows.

First, we have shown that market structure matters in a surprising way if sophisticated consumers face a reading cost: mandating favorable terms must benefit all consumers if sellers are competitive; but cannot benefit and may harm sophisticated consumers if the seller is a monopolist. These effects are mitigated in presence of enough consumers who naïvely believe that fine print contains favorable terms.

We also go further Gabaix and Laibson's (2006) conclusion that competitive sellers may not disclose in the presence of a high enough proportion of naïve consumers: we rather prove that the same result may hold even if all consumers are sophisticated: no seller may find it profitable to disclose, including those offering friendly terms.

Our results may be of some help in the debate about different legal regimes possibly applying to contracts of adhesion. Precisely, we reject the market structure hypothesis as theorized by Kessler (1943), and overturn the traditional economic theory on public intervention proving that rules forcing sellers to disclose may turn out in favor of consumers if sellers are competitive, and may also be socially efficient if the cost of disclosing is lower than the cost of reading. Vice versa, regulation is not desirable if the seller is monopolist and able to disclose; more importantly, even if implemented, such policies would not necessarily turn out consumer protective.

Our analysis for the monopoly also mitigates the difference between salient and non-salient attributes, and rejects the theory that regulation should be limited to the latter category. Although (even naïve) consumers are usually aware about salient

E. D'Agostino, *Contracts of Adhesion Between Law and Economics*,
SpringerBriefs in Law, DOI 10.1007/978-3-319-13114-6_6

attributes, we have shown that no regulation is completely effective if limited to non-salient attributes only: even if forced to offer expensive clauses, the monopolist is able to gain from regulation by charging higher prices to the detriment of consumers. For this reason, we claim that whenever the seller can exploit some market power, every regulation cannot be limited to non-salient and unconscionable attributes, but must be accompanied by a regulation on price and/or other salient (and possibly *conscionable*) attributes.

References

Ahdieh, R.B. "The Strategy of Boilerplate", Michigan Law Review 104, 1033–1074, 2006.
Akerlof, G.A. "The Market for 'Lemons': Quality Uncertainty and the Market Mechanism.", Quarterly Journal of Economics, 84(3), 488–500, 1970.
Armstrong, M. "Interaction between competition and consumer policy", Competition Policy International, 4(1), 97–147, 2008.
Armstrong, M. and Y. Chen "Inattentive Consumers and Product Quality", Journal of the European Economic Association 7(2–3), 411–422, 2009.
Atiyah, P.S. The Rise and Fall of Freedom of Contract, Oxford University Press 1979.
Ayres, I. and E. Rasmusen "Mistake in Contract Law", Journal of Legal Studies 22, 309–343, 1993.
Bagwell, K. and G. Ramey "The Diamond's paradox: A Dynamic Resolution", University of California at San Diego, Economics Working Paper Series 92–45, 1992.
Baird, D. "The Boilerplate Puzzle" Michigan Law Review 104, 933–952, 2006.
Bakos, Y, F. Marotta-Wurgler and D.R. Trossen, "Does anyone read the fine print? Testing a Law and Economic approach to standard form contracts", Journal of Legal Studies 1, 1-35, 2014.
Bebchuk, L. and R. Posner "One-sided Contracts in Competitive Consumer Markets" Michigan Law Review 104, 827–836, 2006.
Benabou, R. "Search, Price Setting and Inflation,", Review of Economic Studies 55(3) 353–376, 1988.
Ben-Shahar, O. "Boilerplate: An Introduction", Michigan Law and Economics Research Paper No. 05–012, 2005.
Ben-Shahar, O. "The Myth of the "Opportunity to Read" in Contract Law", European Review of Contract Law 5(1), 1–28, 2009.
Ben-Shahar, O. and C.E. Schneider, "The Futility of Cost Benefit Analysis in Financial Disclosure Regulation", Law & Economics Working Papers. Paper 100, 2014.
Bernstein, L. "Social Norms and Default rules Analysis", S. Cal. Interdisc. L. Journal 59–90, 1993.
Board, O. "Competition and disclosure", Journal of Industrial Economics 57 197–213, 2009.
Bollinger, B., Leslie, P. and A. Sorensen "Calorie posting in chain restaurants' NBER Working paper No. 15648, 2010.
Che, Y. and A. Choi "Shrink-Wraps: Who Should Bear the Cost of Communicating Mass-Market Contract Terms?", University of Virginia Legal Working Paper Series. Working paper 55, 2009.
Chirelstein, M.A. Concepts and Case Analysis in Law of Contracts, New York: Foundation Press Thomson West, 5th ed., 2006.
Choi, S. and M.G. Gulati "Contract as Statute", Michigan Law Review, 104, 1029–1073, 2006.
Coase, R. "The Problem of Social Cost", The Journal of Law and Economics 3(1), 1–44, 1960.
D'Agostino E. and Seidmann D.J. "Protecting Buyers from Fine Print: Market Structure Matters", MIMEO, 2009.
Davis, K. "The Role of Non-Profits in the Production of Boilerplate", Michigan Law Review, 104 (5), 1075–1103, 2006.

E. D'Agostino, *Contracts of Adhesion Between Law and Economics*,
SpringerBriefs in Law, DOI 10.1007/978-3-319-13114-6

Dawson, P. "Economic Duress—An Essay in Perspective", Michigan Law Review 45(3), 253–290, 1947.
Dawson, P. "Unconscionable Coercion: The German Version", Harvard Law Review 89(6), 1041–1126, 1976.
Diamond, P. "A Model of Price Adjustment", Journal of Economic Theory 3, 156–168, 1971.
Ellison, G. and S.F. Ellison "Search, Obfuscation and Price Elasticities on the Internet", Econometrica 77(2), 427–452, 2009.
Fershtman, C. and A. Fishman "Noisy Search and the Diamond's paradox", Discussion Papers 844, Northwestern University, Center for Mathematical Studies in Economics and Management Science, 1989.
Frances Luce, M., J.R. Bettman and J.W. Payne "Choice Processing In Emotionally Difficult Decisions", Journal of Experimental Psychology: Learning, Memory & Cognition 23, 384–405, 1997.
Friedman, E. "Competition and Unconscionability", American Law and Economics Review 15(2), 443–494, 2013.
Gabaix, X. and D. Laibson "Shrouded Attributes, Consumer Myopia, and Information Suppression in Competitive Markets", Quarterly Journal of Economics 121(2), 505–540, 2006.
Gilmore, G. The Death of Contract, Columbus: Ohio State University Press, 1974.
Gilo D. and A. Porat "The Hidden Roles of Boilerplate and Standard form Contracts" Michigan Law Review 104, 983–1031, 2006.
Gomulkiewicz, R.W. "The License Is the Product: Comments on the Promise of Article 2B for Software and Information Licensing", Berkeley Tech. Law Review 13, 891–930, 1998.
Grether, D., A Schwartz and L. Wilde, "The Irrelevance of Information Overload: An Analysis of Search and Disclosure", Southern California Law Review 59, 277–303, 1986.
Grossman, S.J. "The informational role of warranties and private disclosure about product quality", Journal of Law & Economics 24, 461–483, 1981.
Grossman, S.J. and O.D. Hart, "Disclosure laws and takeover bids", Journal of Finance 35, 323–334, 1980.
Hermalin, B.E., A. Katz and R. Craswell "The Economics of Contract Law", The Handbook of Law and Economics, ed. Steven Shawell and A. Mitchell Polinsky, New York: Elsevier, 2006.
Hill, C.A. and C. King "How Do German Contracts Do as Much with Fewer Words?", Chi.-Kent L. Review 79, 889–926, 2004.
Hillman, R., and J. Rachlinski "Standard-form Contracting in the Electronic Age" New York University Law Review 77, 429–495, 2002.
Holt, C.A. and D.D. Davis "An Examination of the Diamond's paradox: Initial Laboratory Results", Actas de las X Jornadas de Economia Industrial, 1995.
Huck, H. and J. Zhou, "Consumers' Behavioural Biases in Competition: A Survey", MPRA Paper No. 31794, 2011.
Katz, A. "Your Terms or Mine? The Duty to Read the Fine Print in Contracts", Rand Journal of Economics 21, 518–537, 1990.
Kessler, F. "Contracts of Adhesion: Some Thoughts about Freedom of Contract", Columbia Law Review 43, 629–637, 1943.
Korobkin, R. "Bounded Rationality, Standard Form Contracts, and Unconscionability", U.Chi. L. Rev. 70, 1203–1295, 2003.
Lal, R. and C. Matutes "Retail Pricing and Advertising Strategies", Journal of Economics 102, 443–477, 1994.
Leff, A. "Contract as Thing", American U. Law Review, 131–157, 1970.
Levine, D., J. Peck and L. Ye, "Quality disclosure and competition", Journal of Industrial Economics 57, 167–196, 2009.
Llewellin, K. The Common Law Tradition: deciding Appeals, Boston, Toronto: Little, Brown & Co., 1960.
Locke, J. Two Treatises of Social Government, Ed. Laslett P. Cambridge: Cambridge University Press 1988 [reprint].

Maine, H.S. Ancient Law, its Connection with the Early History of Society and its Relation to Modern ideas, London 1861 [reprint, London: J.M. Dent, 1954].

Malhotra, N.K. "Information Load and Consumer Decision Making", Journal of Consumer Research 8, 419–430, 1982.

Marotta-Wurgler, F. "Competition and the Quality of Standard Form Contracts: The Case of Software Licence Agreements", Journal of Empirical Legal Studies 5 447–475, 2008.

Marotta-Wurgler, F. "Does Contract Disclosure Matter?" Journal of Institutional and Theoretical Economics 168, 94–119, 2012.

Mathios, A.D. "The impact of mandatory disclosure laws on product choices: An analysis of the salad dressing market", Journal of Law & Economics 43, 651–677, 2000.

Maxeiner, J.R. "Standard Terms Contracting in the Global Electronic Age: European Alternatives", Yale Journal of International Law 28(1), 2003.

Milgrom, P.R. "Good news and bad news. Representation theorems and applications", Bell Journal of Economics 12, 380–391, 1981.

Nozick, R. Anarchy, State and Utopia, New York: Basic Books, 1974.

Olshavsky, R.W. "Task Complexity and Contingent processing in Decision making: A Replication and Extension", Organizational Behavior and Human Performance 24, 300–316, 1979.

Posner, R.A. Economic Analysis of the Law, 5th ed. New York: Aspen Law & Business, 1998.

Posner, R.A., and A.M. Rosenfield "Impossibility and Related Doctrines in Contract law: An Economic Analysis", Journal of Legal Studies 6, 83–118, 1977.

Priest, G. "A Theory of the Consumer Product Warranty", Yale Law Journal 90, 1297–1352, 1981.

Raiser, L. Das Recht der Allgemeinen Geschäftsbedingungen (1935), Bad Homburg 1961. [reprint].

Rakoff, T. "Contracts of Adhesion: An Essay in Reconstruction" Harvard Law Review 96, 1173–1284, 1983.

Rasmusen, E. "Explaining Incomplete Contracts as the Result of Reading Costs" Advances in Economic Analysis and Policy 1(1), 2001.

Rob, R. "Equilibrium Price Distributions", Review of Economic Studies, 52, 487–504, 1985.

Scheiber, H.N. The State and Freedom of Contract, Stanford Univ. Press, 1998.

Schelling, T.C. The Strategy of Conflict, Harvard University Press, 1960.

Schwartz, A. and L. Wilde, "Imperfect information in markets for contract terms", Antitrust Law Journal 69, 1394–1466, 1983.

Shapiro, C. "Aftermarkets and Consumer Welfare: Making Sense of Kodak", Antitrust Law Journal 63, 483–511, 1995.

Slawson, W.D. "Standard Form Contracts and Democratic Control of Law Making Power", Harvard Law Review 84(3), 529–566, 1971.

Sovern, J. "Toward a New Model of Consumer Protection. The Problem of Inflated Transaction Costs", William and mary Law Review 47(5),1635–1709, 2006.

Stiglitz, J. "Competitivity and the Number of Firms in a Market: Are Duopolies More Competitive Than Atomistic Markets?", IMSSS Technical report no. 476 Stanford University, 1985.

Trebilcock, M.J. The Doctrine of Unequal Bargaining Power: post-Benthamite Economics in the House of Lords, 26 University of Toronto Law Review 359–385, 1976.

Varian, H. "A Model of Sales", American Economic Review 70(4), 651–659, 1980.

Viscusi, W.K. "A note on "lemons" market with quality certification", Bell Journal of Economics 9, 277–279, 1978.

Von Zur Muehlen, P. "Monopolistic Competition and Sequential Search", Journal of Economic Dynamics and Control 2, 257–281, 1980.

Wigmore, J. Evidence in Trials and Common Law, Chadbourn rev. 1981.

White J.J. "Autistic Contracts" Wayne Law Review 45, 2000.

White, J.J., and R.S. Summers Uniform Commercial Code: Revised Article 1 and Amended Article 2: Substance and Process, St. Paul, Minn.: West, 2005.

Wolinsky, A. "True Monopolistic Competition as a Result of Imperfect Information", Quarterly Journal of Economics 101(3), 493–511, 1986.

MIX
Papier aus verantwortungsvollen Quellen
Paper from responsible sources
FSC® C105338

If you have any concerns about our products,
you can contact us on
ProductSafety@springernature.com

In case Publisher is established outside the EU,
the EU authorized representative is:
Springer Nature Customer Service Center GmbH
Europaplatz 3, 69115 Heidelberg, Germany

Printed by Libri Plureos GmbH
in Hamburg, Germany